Twilight Till Dawn

LORD R. HANDYSIDE

authorHOUSE®

AuthorHouse™ UK
1663 Liberty Drive
Bloomington, IN 47403 USA
www.authorhouse.co.uk
Phone: UK TFN: 0800 0148641 (Toll Free inside the UK)
*   UK Local: 02036 956322 (+44 20 3695 6322 from outside the UK)*

Published by AuthorHouse 06/30/2020

ISBN: 978-1-7283-5393-7 (sc)
ISBN: 978-1-7283-5392-0 (e)

Despatchers:

This is my chance to thank all of the people that have helped me in my endeavour to produce this book.

- Eloise Benjamin
- Aaaron Evans
- Lewis Burgess
- Nick & Paola Sawle
- Gary
- Jessica White

Contents

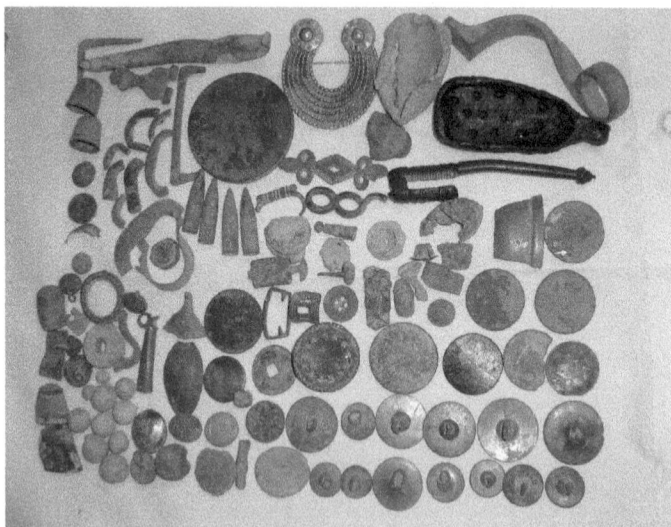

Detecting Gt Chis. Nov 2005

1

The Beginning

The beginning, where to start. You might say, from the beginning but defining the beginning, is easier said than done. So, I think we'll start during my last year of school. I went to a mid-range public school, mid-range meaning price-wise, that was military-orientated. I quite liked the square bashing and we marched everywhere, so on the whole, I enjoyed school life; especially, when we were on the shooting range. When you first go to the school, you practice with 22s but from the age of 13, we went on to the beloved 303s – a fabulous rifle, the Lee Enfield.

Throughout my school life, like most boys, I had collected various things, such as cigarette cards, stamps, butterflies, bird eggs etc… but nothing really grabbed my enthusiasm. The interest fell away from these as the years went on. At school I was a member of the Anglian Club and the Chess Club, for which by the time I had left, I was joint champion at the school. The other thing I did in my spare time, was I joined the home maintenance course, which I did throughout my entire academic career. Also I did the bee keeping course which was run by the school groundsman. Incidentally, later in life I became a bee farmer. This came to serve me well later on, because at the end of the last term, I was hit with a bombshell – that particular year, there were only 5 of us going to the recruitment office. Some of the other boys had fathers who were accountants and merchant bankers, and so this was the wrong school for them. The five of us arrived at the recruitment office and in true military style, it was carried out in alphabetical order, which meant that I was third on the list. We all still had to go through the written and physical exam. So, on completion, the colour sergeant came into the waiting room and announced to all of us, that we had all passed and he would give us our options and as we got them, we went into the next room to sign up for the armed forces.

Starting with the first two, they went to Sandhurst, then it should have been my turn but he went to 4 and 5 first. So, I was bewildered but then as the last boy left the room, he turned to me and said the Medical Officer (MO) wanted a word with you. So, I went back into the MOs office and as I walked in, he handed me a book and he said to me to read page 10 in your own time; which I did. I was thinking he had found some disease, and this made me worried. I didn't understand what was going on and then he started acting in an agitated manner, almost shouting at me, before telling me quickly to read page 11 as fast as you can. Which I did. He then just took the book from me and instructed me to return to the waiting room. After a couple of minutes, the colour sergeant came into the waiting room and stood in front of me, and said that I would not be going to any of the officer training colleges. I was told that I could join any service I liked but would never be allowed to go above private. I was bewildered and then I asked why, as I thought I had passed all the tests. He said, it was because of my stammer, as you can't be in the position to give orders during a conflict. So, I simply said, no thank you, and left the room. I joined the other lads on the coach back to school.

About 2-3 weeks later, at the end of term, I left and all the other boys were off to summer camp. They would then go home for the summer holidays. But that left me high and dry, as I hadn't considered doing anything else. So, I arrived home and although I was sure my father was disappointed, he seemed okay about the whole thing; seeing as it wasn't my fault. He started to look around at his friends at his club and eventually came up with a bricklaying apprenticeship with a company called Buckingham's, whose director was a friend of his. This was where the home maintenance courses I had carried out at school had paid off; as I knew I was good at bricklaying from then. So, I took my apprenticeship and ended up in Willesden College. This went on for 4 years and although I wasn't really happy with the situation, I could not leave, as I had already signed up for the apprenticeship. Then I was at home and one of my friends had just finished their tour in N. Ireland and was on leave. We were talking about the whole situation and what else I could do. I knew I would not go into an office, as I was an outdoor type person. I liked the freedom. and I was always interested in animals. Then towards the end of his leave, he told me that he had written to a company for a position in their company as a trainee taxidermist. I thought no more of it, but after 2-3 weeks, I received a letter from Roland Wards – the best taxidermist in the world. I went to the interview and they offered me the position. I had to wait until the revision for City & Guilds bricklaying had started, as this was the earliest I could leave. Which I did and I went to work for Roland Wards, the best taxidermist in the world. But that's a whole new story.

So, onto how my passion for metal detecting started. After some years, I left Wards and I opened my own building business. This was a time when everybody started buying their own houses, it was the start of the boom period and I was getting a lot of work. Small to start with and in the course of carrying out work on people's houses, I started to find coins. Having that basic collecting instinct, I just started hoarding them until one day, I found a George III Cartwheel 2 pence piece (1897). So that sparked my interest, as I had to look up what it was and research it. Then 2-3 weeks later, whilst clearing out the roof space of a house, I found a small tinned box, which used to be for fisherman friend sweets. On opening the box, I discovered 6 silver Thruppence pieces. So, now the interest really took hold. I went straight out to buy a coin book, which was the first one I had bought in 1972. I still have this. By now, I was asking the customers whether they had any old coins and once the decimalisation came through, people started handing me all their old imperial coins. These were mounting up quite fast, so I bought the plastic type folders with the pockets and just put the coins into each folder. I put all the pennies in one sleeve and all the ha'pennies another. But in no real sense of a collection, I was just hoarding them. There was no structure to the collection until one day, whilst building an extension in Edgware, I needed to construct a land beam and I needed a rebar cage to form the foundation. I knew of a gypsy fellow (Marty), who lived in a house in Watford, and I got him to make the cage for me. Then I started a little friendship with him and in talking to him, he told me that he had a friend who would go metal detecting around the Watford area and was finding all sorts of coins. This interested me immensely. So, he said he would have a word with this friend to determine some good site to go to, if I were to buy a metal detector – which I did.

At first, I could go around parks and picnic areas and found relatively modern coins, which I kept. Until, that Christmas, I took my new detector up to a Roman posting station, on the top of Brockley Hill. I knew this because I had seen the plaque on a hoarding that the council had erected in the field. Although it was overgrown, I had already seen where it was. So, I got there and the ground was frozen solid. I managed to work around the base of an oak tree and managed to find and discover two small A4 Roman coins, which were totally unidentifiable, by their size and by the fact that they were bronze. But now, I was hooked and started to buy books to read about the history of these coins and where I might find the various types.

From this point I then purchased a fabulous machine, a Compass, which was a bit heavy to use for long periods but the depth the machine could pick up was staggering. This machine would take 12 batteries to power it. That was only one night's session, at a cost of £9 a time, this was expensive, especially if you were going out two or three times a week. But when the Compass went wrong, I was forced into getting another machine but in hindsight and with the knowledge I now possess, it was only the search coil that had broken and was a great machine for day time. But for Night Hawking, you would need a Switch it on and go, and a light weight machine.

I think I should explain what knight hawkers are; in a nutshell, they are people who go metal detecting at night without permission. Maybe I should also inform you about what I call the gangs back in the 60s when detecting took off, people formed groups which mainly was controlled by the size of the vehicle used so 4 or 5. I went out with a number of them. I will go through them from the top downwards. I first met Scully through an advert he had in one of the detecting magazines. He buys all sorts of artefacts and I had 1 or 2 artefacts and a detector to sell in my area. I had been given bad prices for example, I had a brand new fisher still in the box and down here they would only pay £350 but Scully offered a minimum of 3100 which made the journey worthwhile. So I went to Scunthorpe to his house and on conclusion of our business I was very happy. He told me in future we could meet at a site he called the Cliff which is about two thirds of the way there so from then on I did just that. The next one down is the Norfolk gang which was headed up by 'Old Boy'; a lot of the Essex gangs meet there as they all know of him. Down a bit more, is Birmingham headed up by 'Postie', this gang went mainly in the day as land owners are more accommodating in that area. Personally, it was quite nice to go in daylight now and then and hence we have stayed friends to this day. Next we are onto heathrow, this gang is headed up by 'Paddy'. Then the second gang is headed up by 'Oblivious' in Slough. Following on in Iver the gang is headed up by 'Macgyver' and then Watford's gang is headed up by 'Carrottop' and Kings Langley by 'Rat'. Then Garston is headed by 'Trotsky'; now we go to Bushey ran by 'I-tie'. Now we move onto Essex where gang number one is 'Gazza' then 'Bootsy' heads up gang number two, gang number 3 is run by 'Pig', gang number four by 'Nutter' and gang five by the 'Little shit'. Then, last but not least is Jiffy in Aylesbury; and that's all folks.

My next purchase was the loved by all, Tesoro Silver Sabre, which seemed to suit my needs. It was a good, all round, lightweight machine, but there seemed to be something missing from its performance. It just wasn't right. After having various conversations with other Night Hawkers, it came to light that the search head that came with the machine was total crap. I was advised to send the machine to Pentechnic which I did and once the machine had returned from Pentechnic I discovered they rewired the search coil properly and found the Silver Sabre to be a brilliant machine, I was now really happy with my new machine. When you tell people that you're a metal detectorist, one of the first questions they ask is what the best thing is that you've ever found. Now this depends on your point of view, if by that you mean what's the most valuable thing you've found, then that would be quite easy to answer. It would usually be one of the gold coins but in my point of view, that's not the case. This is because some of the broaches I've found, which I consider to be amongst the best items I've found, carry a value of about £40.

Before we go too much further, I'd like to say a few words about metal detecting. Detecting is partly skill, but mainly luck. I have put this to the test on a few occasions, whereby I would purposely walk behind somebody else and have them walk behind me to see whether anything was found or missed. There is no doubt that there is skill in learning the different subtleties of the sound created by different signals, which of course is learnt with time and practice. There is of course an alternative and that's to adopt the approach as done by many beginners, to dig everything but where you walk, to be on the safe side, and if it's over a good signal; that is the lucky part. I can give you one example of this, 'Carrottop' and yours truly went to a site at Ashwell, this is a medieval site, which we believed was a fairground in its day, rather like a modern car boots sale. There are two areas on this field, where you find the hammered pennies and the cut halves and quarters; the latter two are harder to find as they are smaller. Anyway we started in the far top corner, from the hedge going out into the field, we were working parallel to each other and when we reached the furthest point we would turn to come back but crossover and we would do the same again when we reached the hedge. So we methodically worked this area and as we were doing so every now and again, 'Carrottop' would shout out "I've got one!", as we were doing this I matched him signal for signal. When we had finished and got back to the car we were going through the evening's finds, then 'Carrottop' said "I've got ten pennies' '. I had ten signals, six halfs four quarters. So this demonstrates, there was more skill in my finds, but he was the lucky one. Maybe had we not crossed over, I would have found some of the whole pennies as well.

Detecting Rectory 21.10.07

2

The Adventure Begins

The first adventure happened on the Alban's with Marty. We were working the theatre field at the far end, up the bank near the woods, where the previous night I had got a pair of Roman bronze rings from the same location. Suddenly, the farmer's pick up truck came roaring onto the field, although the headlights were on us, I knew from experience that he could not see us. Fortunately, we were about 40 feet away from the edge of the woods and the natural reaction is to run, which we did, straight into the woods.

I knew the woods were the old Roman boundary but what I didn't know was that the old Roman wall is still there at that point in the woods. Also interestingly, the woods are mainly made up in saplings of about three inches in diameter. In the panic to get away from the farmer, I go sailing off the wall only to realise I am ten feet in the air and the only way to go is down.

In desperation I grabbed at a sapling and believe or not this took my weight and I slid down it like a fire man's pole. The drop shook me up badly, but the only casualties were the zip on my Barbour, my hands and my arse from hitting the ground.

Marty managed to stop himself from making this leap of faith and was now on his hands and knees, peering over the edge. I handed him up my machine and climbed back up this bloody wall. We went back five feet to the woods edge, had a smoke and watched the farmer rally round the field in his truck until he left. When he did, so did we.

A few nights later, Marty and I were on the market field alone. Now this field being very narrow, if anybody drove up the Roman road, the practice was to just lie down. We happened to be close to the main road. where there is a wire fence and on the other side, this wire is a large drop down an embankment. A car came down the road and had to stop in order to open the gate, as we were near the edge of the field we ran to the boundary where we stopped and laid down, as opposed to going over it because of the drop. When we were in the furrows of the ploughing, my machine was out in front of me, chattering like women in a hairdressers. I thought I had damaged my machine by hitting the ground so hard. So, while lying there dead still and pinned down waiting for the gate light to go out, I decided to check on my machine. I lifted my head to see if it was cracked or broken and as the chattering stopped, I could see something glistening in the light; a Seal Matrix, just lying there.

This was the first one I had ever got, and it was in lovely condition and it was well worth the panic and the pain of throwing yourself at the ground at high speed and I said to myself, "lovely." For the rest of the night, no problems or panics, it was an alright night actually, where I walked off with about 40 coins or so, with some of them being silver.

My time as a metal detector had grown with my friend Marty, whom I had started with, but now has died due to a heart illness. I continued to nighthawk, doing the Albans and the Roast by myself at night. Then late one evening, I was going on the Roast when I bumped into foureyes, who gave me a fright because he pulled up in the lay by where I had just left my car!

I got talking to him and Night Hawkers being Night Hawkers we struck up a friendship. Foureyes had his own little gang of hawkers who didn't like the idea of a newcomer in the group, but they would not do the "Albans" as they considered it too hot. Foureyes wanted to do the "Albans" but nobody would go with him! Low and behold he had a new ally and we started to work the Albans together fairly regularly along with other sites. Foureyes remained loyal to his group, so the consequence was that when they went out, I was on my own again.

One night, however, on the Albans, we were working the theatre field until the very early hours, so we decided to go down on to the market field. It was a full moon and we should have known better, but we didn't care. As some of you may know, to get to the market field from the theatre field you have to cross the estate road, which happens to be the Roman road. From the theatre field down to the road, the embankments are about five feet high. I was in front and started to go down the embankment, which was wet, muddy and slippery, and yeah, you guessed it, I travelled down this slope on my heels. I managed to maintain my balance, remained upright and ended up on the road. Unfortunately, I also hit the rear wheel of a pushbike, who was pedaling along the road with no light on. I suspect it was one of the farm labourers, who in a spectacular piece of control, wobbled and swerved but maintained his balance. I stood there and watched in amazement, getting ready to clamber back up the embankment while Foureyes was on the verge of coming down but to my pure astonishment the cyclist didn't stop or say anything just kept going. Foureyes came down the embankment and we both ran across the road and travelled towards the trees to have a quick smoke and discuss what had just happened.

At this point, we should have left the site, we knew it was only a matter of time before one of the farm staff would be out looking for us. So, we decided to work our way down the field, bearing in mind it's a full moon and you can see right across the fields. We, like the dynamic duo, decided to go and work the roadside. This is where you get a lot of silver.

We were no more than 20 yards from the road and about 100 yards along the field. I was in front of Foureyes when suddenly he hit me on the back and said, "hit the deck", which we both did promptly. Foureyes had heard the tires on the gravel road that the farmer was now coming down in his pickup with lights off and he said get ready to run. We watch the silhouette of the truck come towards us as they were looking for us on the field. We knew they didn't know where we were or even if we were still there even, so we stayed and stayed still.

The truck slowly went past us but due to the field not being flat and the fact that the farmer was aware of our presence, but not knowing where and who, he didn't see us. Then suddenly one of the men on the back of the pickup banged on the roof, brake lights came, on and men were jumping off the back and we were up and running.

Foureyes who was younger and fitter than me was in front but was only just about half way across the field when I realised, I had dropped my prized stainless steel trowel. I stopped and turned around with the intention of going back and getting it but looked up only to realise that there were more farm workers then I had estimated. If it had been only one or two men then I would've braved it. I decided to run again but I now have to run harder to catch up with Foureyes and to get away from the ensuing mob by running at full speed or as fast as you could do in a heavy Wellington coat with a metal detector in your hand. I switched the machine off and pulled the headphones off my head which I dropped, and they are now trailing behind me and my legs. As you can imagine this was a bit of a hindrance, so I grabbed the cable and tried to pull them, not forgetting that I'm still full speed. This was fine until the headset had reached my knees because as they came through my knees they just crashed them.

By the time I reached the edge of the field there was a trail of broken headphones across the field and all I was left with was a bit of wire. Along the edge of that field there is no hedge but by the trees the fence wire is more accessible. However the down side of this, is that on the other side of the wood is a huge drop. But by the choice of my run across the field which was at an angle to the tree we were both heading for the same spot but Foureyes route was straight and even though I stopped to mess with the headset and all of that, we got to the fence at the same time but not the same spot. I got through the wire easy, but Foureyes chose the hard way and now he's sliding down the bank. Now, we are both at the bottom of the ditch out of sight of the chasing mob, we went back on ourselves in the ditch to make it to the gateway. The field which has a double gateway hidden by trees and so we decided to make it there and plot our next move.

While we stand and regain our breath, we watch what the mob were doing. They were now all back in and on the Toyota Hi Ace, which was heading the way we were heading. We continued with our route through the little wood and lent over the fence which fences off number three only to see the mob trucks with all lights now coming down the edge of the field. We then doubled back on ourselves through the wood over the gate towards the river. Fortunately the river had been drying for some reason and had been for the last couple of years. This was our saviour because if it hadn't and the water had been flowing, our escape via this route would have been closed and our capture a safe bet.

We both ran across the semi dry riverbed up the other bank to barbed wire fencing. Being a six footer, I got straight over but Foureyes being a short arse, had major problems getting over this hurdle. I just kept going and Foureyes once through the fence, went his own way. I knew he was going more or less the same way as me to end up in the corner of the roundabout field. So as I was running through the wood I was startled at a fox, which unbelievably was now running alongside me with a "what are we running from" look on his face. I hit the corner of the roundabout field and at this point the Redbourne Road is straight in front of you, the pub hotel is on your left. The choices were to walk along the Redbourne Road for about half a mile this was not very safe considering that there is an angry mob after you all, or going into a pub ground with no means of escape and just waiting out. Either way my car was miles away.

I chose to go along the river embankment towards the main road at the far end of the field because at the side of the river, there was a hedge which meant I had some cover so where the river goes under the road, I could hop up onto the main road, cross it and move across the footpath opposite. To my luck it was overgrown which again gave me cover to aid my escape. I then wrapped my machine with my barbour coat and hid it in the undergrowth. I then returned to the main road and walked over the river via the bridge and along the road for 50 yards before I entered a housing estate where my car was parked.

Upon reaching the car I took off my wellingtons and put on my shoes. I now look like a normal punter and not a hawker, and with that I felt safe. I waited for 30 minutes for Foureyes to appear but no sign of him. I drove out of the estate to the other end of the footpath, got my machine and coat and then went back to where I was originally parked and waited a bit longer.

By now, an hour had passed but still no sign of Foureyes and I knew no way he had been caught as he had too much head start over the pursuing mob. I then took it upon myself to drive around and try and find him or at least what happened to him. After a few minutes driving around slowly I found myself heading down the Redbourne Road towards the entrance of the pub hotel. Suddenly Foureyes jumped over the hedge in just his shirtsleeves. I stop and he jumped in. By this time, we reached the entrance of the pub hotel car park we intended to swing round and roar off but Foureyes said he had hidden his gear in there.

Just as I was about to turn into the pub there was a set of lights on the car coming up the drive from the pub. Being three in the morning, I knew it could not have been patrons of the pub so I kept on going up the Redbourne Road. I looked in my rear-view mirror and it was the Toyota Hi Ace with the mob in it and on it. The farmer and his crew are now behind me and followed me for about half a mile and then turned off into the estate. We continued to the end of the Redbourne Road, parked up, had a smoke and Foureyes told me what happened to him.

When he left the riverbank, he headed towards the pub hotel at an angle, he started to walk up the driveway to get onto the road when he saw the mob, so he hid in the bushes. Then he worked his way to the pub entrance where there was the perfect hiding place. This was a double signboard set up in a v shape. He then clambered into the signboard, got out of his hawking uniform and clined back out. This meant he had to go down to the main road but the mob was circling around which meant they had him pinned down and didn't know it but it also meant that he had to hedgehop and eventually made it into the field where he jumped out on me. After our smoke we returned to the pub entrance, retrieved Foureyes gear and sped off via the back roads to Bedfordshire.

Another incident whilst out with Foureyes we went up to boffin to work that site as we had done for some time. At this site the resident farmer doesn't chase you in a land rover pick up, he uses an off-road quad bike. On this particular night we were on top of the hill and there were about eight or so guys from another gang of hawkers working their way down the hill towards the main road.

Suddenly a police car pulled into the layby opposite. The officer driving the car got out of the vehicle with a megaphone in his hand and like General Patton, he stood there and shouted you've got five minutes to get off this field before I come after you. He then calmly got back into his police car drove off down the road.

Well we were at the top of the field and the other gang we were about halfway down the slope of the hill. From where we were, we had a great view of what was unfolding. The other gang were running around in all sorts of directions with no apparent plan of where they were running to or from. This was a highly amusing situation because where we were, we were super safe laughing at them running around like blue arsed flies running from themselves.

The Odd Things You Bump Into

Whilst on one of the 'unhot' Peterborough sites with my oppo Foureyes on this one site the access lane comes down on the side of the field and terminates in a small car park in front of the railway crossing. This is where we were parked. Immediately opposite the gate of the field was a small copse of 30-40 trees in a circular shape. We had got there fairly early but after about an hour, cars kept coming down the lane and going to the copse. At first, we kept hiding from every car that came down the lane, but after a while, we figured it must be kids out shagging or just messing about, so we paid no attention to it.

An hour passed and we noticed there was a fire in the

copse. This fire over a short period of time got bigger and bigger and bigger. In the meantime, the music being played by these kids had got louder and louder, and girls were screaming, and people were running about making a lot of noise. The noise level had gotten so loud and the fire had gotten so big it actually lit the field that Foureyes and I were working in. It was like working in daylight. The flames were 40-50 feet in the air, that's how big the fire was.

As you may realise, being scared easily is not natural, so during one of our smoke breaks, we decided to stay and work in the field until the Babylon arrived. We didn't want to leave the field whilst the rave was still on, as it meant we had to pass them to get out and away. So, the decision was to stay and work on until they had left, which was about four in the morning.

When you consider that the closest houses are on the side of the field, which is less than half a mile away, we were amazed that nobody was called out. No police, no firemen, no members of a public body, just no one. What's going on here then, we thought and instead, laughed about it all the way home.

Detecting South Mims 11.06

3

Trapped

One night whilst working the theatre field on the Alban's, Foureyes and I worked in a similar spot to where Marty and I had worked previously. By the tree that stands all alone on the field, was a good area for Celtic coinage. We could see that there were quite a number of other hawkers down the slope working that area. From the position we were in we had a commanding view of the area and we could see the farmer coming along the road with his lights off. The others along the slope did not see him, but we definitely could.

Foureyes and I had linked up and chatted about which way we were going to run, as I didn't want to run over his arse when the time came. So, we had a smoke and watched what the farmer was doing.

The farmer had now parked behind the Roman theatre and was on foot. He emerged from behind the theatre up onto the field where the alarm was raised and there were bodies scattering everywhere. The three bodies were heading up the field towards us. One of them turned out to be 'Carrottop' who I was about to meet for the first time.

When they reached us they stopped and had a chat and watched with us the chaos that was transpiring on the field below with the Irene farmer and some of the hard-core night hawkers.

After the usual pleasantries of hello how are you where do you come from, our escape route would have been top of the field through the gate behind us but the silhouette of two people in that very gateway had scuttled that idea. The situation has now become serious as it was our arse in a jam and not somebody else's.

Foureyes and I broke away from the others and decided to go across the field at an angle. In amongst the confusion and the mass of bodies, the choice of who to grab worked in our favour as there were just so many people running about.

We left the field and went home and heard a few days later from 'Carrottop', that one of the guys that went with him that night; it was his first night out metal detecting and low and behold he got caught.

About a week later on the same field in the very similar situation the police had arrived in numbers to try and surround the field. Foureyes and I were off there like cats from the first sight of the Babylon. We used all the tried and tested escape routes to get away but somebody was and had followed us.

There were about 12 to 15 hawkers that night on the field but we knew once we'd gone across the field, the road and into the park we would be safe, as per usual, we stopped for a smoke but the person on our trail had caught up to us.

This pursuer turned out to be 'Little shit' who thought he was following a couple of members from his gang, but this was wrong and he was in a bit of the spot. Because in following us we had ended up where our car was parked and not to where his car was parked right across the other side of site. When Foureyes and I got out of the uniform we offered him a lift back to his car which he appreciated, and it was because he was a night hawker.

Another incident at the time that was a real downer was after we travelled all the way to Mildenhall, which was a long way from home. Foureyes came up with a great idea about where to park the car as you may know that for most sites this is a problem. The idea was going into the field, parked the car behind the hedge close to the gate hoping nobody would be there. So, in theory, this was the perfect plan. Once we reached an extremely big hill behind Mildenhall we started to look for a suitable gateway with a big hedge, which we found on the brow of the hill. This seemed like the perfect spot.

I drove onto the field to turn the car around so it's facing outwards for a quick getaway and parked alongside the hedge. The view from up there was spectacular, as the field was in stubble and was firmer underfoot.

So, from where we were plotted up the hill falls at a small decline and then drops off rapidly. It always amazes me how farmers plough the slopes of the angles they have to get their machinery and so without tripping or falling down their fields.

I was standing by the foot of the car getting on the hawkers uniform Barbour jacket, woolly hat, fingerless gloves and yes you guessed it, our assault course running shoes known as Wellington Boots.

The whole time we were rigging up we could hear in the distance coming of farm machinery a low rumbling noise. We paid no mind to it because we figured it was a long way away. Well suddenly then we lit up with the light that you could have lit Wembley Stadium with. There were some of us dressed, some others semi-dressed but all frozen still in the beam of light which reminded me of being in the presence of the UFO. You must understand, it was pitch black, we were on the top of this hill and what could you do, except for panic. It was pandemonium, people trying to get gear off and jamming into their boots. There were arms and legs everywhere.

Behind the unidentified flying light, to total horror was a combine harvester with cutting things at the front whizzing round, trundling towards us. With one click of the central locking button, we were all in the car. Fortunately, we had not closed the gate. We started the car and got out of the field faster than a gallon of unleaded in a fuel crisis. That was another night swinging stick ruined.

Accidental Finds

I have quite often found items almost accidentally. On one occasion, I went to the Cow Roast and it was late autumn/early winter. I drove round to see if the fields had been ploughed and looking from the main road, I could see the field was very dark – an indication that it had indeed been ploughed. This was of course at twilight, so I drove round onto the smaller roads and parked near the sites. I walked onto the site and by the time I had reached the actual field, the moon was up and was quite bright. I walked onto the field and it was heavily ploughed, so not suitable for detecting. But I stood on the edge of the field and I noticed a change in colour two thirds of the way up, so I thought maybe the farmer had flattened the top bit, leaving the rest for the next day. I then walked right across the field, standing on the top of the farrow until I reached the end. but when I got there, I realised what he had done is he had raked it and not ploughed it at all. The part of the field he had left, didn't produce anything, so I was standing on the first or last furrow, contemplating on what to do. I looked down at my feet in order to step off onto the flatted area and in the moonlight, I could see a turtle broach. Now I had completed just going over the field anyway, but I bent down and picked up the broach. The broach was complete but the enamelling and the eyes were gone. The broach had all four legs, its tail and head and everything apart from the pin being missing. Nevermind, as 95% of broach's pins are missing, because the body is bronze and the pins are steel (rusts away and breaks off). So, I picked it up and had a second thought about going on the field and instead, turned around and went home.

I then phoned a dealer the next day and he gave me £140 for it. Had the enamelling and eyes been intact, it would have been £600. Even though this broach does not come into the category of the best item I've found, it was still nice.

On another instance, I was on the market field on the Auburn's and I had only just got onto the field when the security light on the gate came on. So, I ran to the edge of the field and laid down against the barbed wire fence. As I was lying there, waiting for the farmer to drive off, once they went through the gate, the light turned off again. The whole time my machine was beeping in my ear constantly. At first, I thought it was the barbed wire causing it, so I moved the head slightly away from the wire, but the sound continued. So, when I felt it was safe, I got up onto my knees and then investigated around the search area. Just lying there on the top, in the first rut of the field, I found a Cil matrix. On investigation, it turned out to be the Seal of the Archbishop.

On another occasion, we were on a known medieval site with 'Bootsy' and we were working our way from the bottom of the hill up towards the road, when someone with two Alsatians came into view on the road. 'Bootsy' and I were fairly near the edge of the field and ran over and laid down near the hedge. Once again, my machine was chattering. when the danger had passed, I checked the area and found a ring seal. That was all I had found that night, unfortunately. That's the way it goes

On another occasion, whilst on my own, on a roman villa site, at Mill End, I was searching the area behind the car park when I saw the farmers headlights come into the top of the field. So, I ran and laid down beside the fence at the car park, always in the first furrow, which is the best place to lie down. Now this time, there was no noise from the machine, but I laid there until the farmer had left. I stood up, adjusted myself and put the machine head on the floor and after moving slightly, I got the welcoming sound of a beep. I looked under the head and picked up a broach (a fibular). It was in absolutely excellent condition, with the bronze pin and was in working order. I don't know how someone could have lost it. This I consider to be one of my best finds. I sold that one to a neighbour and a friend, who was interested.in it.

Hadrian Denari

4

The Samtone Incident

One night 'Little shit' and I decided to go to a site called Samtone. Once again, the site was a troublesome site as parking was a real bitch and the site was hot.not just hot but HOT!

We parked in the entrance of an electrical substation about four fields away; entering the site from behind. The trouble with this route is that there were a lot of obstacles en route, such as rivers and fences. There are a few fields that make up the site but the one field where we were aiming for, was long, thin and ran parallel to the road. Entering the field from the back meant that we had a fence between us and the field. What the farmer had done was he had put up a double barbed wire fence and the top wires were far higher than normal. This made access extremely difficult; but more to the point it made an escape actually impossible when in a hurry

We negotiated the fence and hence because we were standing in the field, I triumphantly turned on my machine and stepped out. With the first swing of my stick a signal beeped and I found a Roman coin within a Celtic site, which is quite normal. I had another three Roman coins and by now I was 5 to 6 feet into the field. I got a signal from my fifth coin on that evening and bent down to pick it up. As I did, I got a handful of mud clenched in my hand. I swung the machine over the hole but sadly there was no signal. This meant I had the object in my hand.

At that moment, 'Little Shit' shouted 'Run!', even though he was still at the edge of the field and hadn't even started to detect. I looked up to see two cars travelling in opposite directions, who had come face-to-face with each other and stopped directly in front of us on the road.

Still with the mud and coin in my hand I turned and ran towards the fence. Upon reaching the fence, I realised that I had one hand full of mud and my machine in the other, so I dumped the mud and what it concealed into my pocket, unplugged my headset from the machine and threw it over the fences. I negotiated both fences and what a bastard that was. I easily caught 'Little Shit' and the others up, as they were not running at top speed but just a fast jog. It also helped that about half way across the field they stopped and looked back to see what was happening and at this point 'Little Shit' was jogging backwards.

The two cars were still there, and the occupants were standing in the road. How many of them were there? I am not sure, as all you could see were the shadows moving in the headlights. We were unable to make out what and who they were, so we were prudent and proceeded to leave the site. On the way home, while travelling down the A12, we saw there was an all-night truck stop café. We pulled in for a cup of tea and something to eat, as at this time of night as it was too late to go onto another site, so we instead decided to go home. Whilst in the café, we were sitting around discussing the events of the night and the fact that 'Little Shit' had not even turned on his machine. He asked me what did you get? I then plunged my hand into my pocket and scooped out this huge pile of mud and dumped on the table. To my huge elation, a perfect Gold Quarter Stator broke free from the mud and rolled across the table to the group heckling "you jammy bastard." Although the coin itself is not worth much it certainly made my night and made a wonderful addition to my collection. We sat around in the café and had been there for just about an hour when two more cars poured into the car park and as it turns out these two cars were the same two cars that had scared us off the field. These cars contained two separate gangs that had bumped into each other and had stopped for a chat. This was a stupid thing to do and was born out by the fact that they had been chased off the site themselves just half an hour later.

Personally, I didn't know any of them but as per usual, 'Little Shit' did.

Archaeologists

Where to start? There are mainly two types of archaeologists, there is the majority that have the attitude that unless you're an archaeologist, you should not be allowed to handle or own any artefacts whatsoever. They had the attitude that it all belongs to them. But I'd like to point out that this is our heritage and people collecting the various things that they do, keeps it in circulation for everybody to appreciate. Even if somebody has a collection all of their life, the chances are that when they die, it will go back into circulation via the dealers. This attitude of locking everything up in vaults in museums, in my opinion, is wrong. However, I have met one or two that are quite 'live and let live' and don't mind metal detectors or antique collectors. However you need to remember that they are a minority and most of them will even ban antique furniture if they could! I appreciate the fact that they've been to college and have a degree, which brands them as an archaeologist, but without making it too simple, when you look at that course, it's basically learning to file the items the way the establishment wants it doing. A good example of this, is the popular program called Time Team. It is shown on many occasions how they get it wrong, because a lot of what they say is their opinion. So, there's a lot of guesswork involved.

All in All a Good Day

I wanted to buy an old Tosorro Gold Sabre. The reason being that this machine had a function called all metal, which meant that you could just flick a switch and the discrimination would be turned off. Althoguh you can turn the discrimination off on most machines, it means retuning the machine after to go back into normal mode. The reason I wanted this machine with this function was because over near Heathrow Airport, there is a site called Waycock Hill. This site is predominantly a Roman site but in the corner of one of the fields, there was a scattered Celtic hoard. The conditions of the soil there were very peculiar and also, another metal detectorist, who seemed to think it was his site, in spite, had scattered small washers and tacks over the

31

whole area. Now 'Paddy' had told me that he had found a way to search the site using a Gold Sabre. It just means digging every single signal and working your way through the rubbish and this seems to pay off. So, I telephoned all the dealers that I knew, and they wanted £200-300 for this old machine but I knew that if you tried to sell that machine to them, they would only allow you about £50. After checking all the detectorists I knew and they came up with nothing, I had to broaden my search. I got in touch with 'Postie'. He didn't know of anybody at the time but said he would ask around. After about 3 days, he telephoned me and said that he had someone that wanted to sell a machine but said it was expensive, as he wanted £150. I told him that if the machine was good, I would be prepared to pay that. 'Postie' did not know the machine, so was unable to vouch for its worthiness. So, we agreed to meet up somewhere, so that I could test the machine for myself. He agreed to meet up and in order to be fair, we would meet approximately halfway. So, he would travel down and I would travel up. The only decent site that fitted the criteria, which was also a difficult site to work on, was Number 10. Now this site had a number because back in the early days, there was a lot of competition and rivalry between the various gangs. Our gang gave certain sites numbers. Because the Essex crowd tended to meet up in the pub before leaving for the night, it was handy that we could just talk to our group and say to meet on whatever number. The others wouldn't have a clue where we were going. So, 'Postie' drove down to Number 10, which was just north of Woodstock. I drove up and went through Woodstock to a garage just outside, where you needed to turn off for Number 10. 'Postie' drove down to this garage. From the garage to Birmingham, it's pretty much a straight road the entire way; making it very convenient. We met at the garage and I showed him the way round to Number 10. He had not been to the site before nor did he know of it. We parked up and went onto the site at the top of the field, which is on a hill, with the road also at the top. On the plateau, there had been a Roman villa. So, you knew you could get a few Roman coins on the top. This is where we started. I pointed out the layout of the field, which was in daylight, most unusual, and explained to 'Postie' where you would find different things; what we would call hotspots. I started searching along the top and 'Postie' started on the slope going down. He had gone to an area that I had pointed, where he could find a broach or two. I worked along the top and found a denarius before I then moved to go down the slope to go alongside the hedge. I had found silver units on that slop before. As I went down, sure enough, I found one. I carried on to the bottom of the field and as I turned to come up, I found another Denarii. I came back up the hill, towards 'Postie'. He was waving to me, so I went to see what was up, he wanted lunch. So, we went back to my land rover, which was parked on the field and we'd brought flasks and sandwiches. After we had finished, I walked about half way down the field and started to search in the middle, where I knew that previously 'Carrottop' had found a Stator. I was searching this area for about an hour or so and I found a Quarter Stator. I was just going backwards and forwards across the field and as I was at the far end of the field, I turned to do the journey back, I glanced up and 'Postie' was waving at me again. So, I walked over to him and although he had found three broaches, he hadn't found a single coin. But I wasn't surprised, as it was a difficult site to work. Anyway, he said that he had had enough and wanted to go home. I said I would have the machine and paid him and off he went. I carried on, as this was only about 3pm. I worked my way down to the bottom of the field to another hotspot and I found two more silver units. By now, it was just becoming dusk and although I could have carried on into the night, I'd been at it since about 10am and quite frankly, I'd had enough. I went home.

Whilst we're still on the subject of Number 10, this site was shown to me by the 'I-tie' and 'Chocsky'. They had taken me to Number 10 and in those days, we always searched it in the day. The 'I-tie' and 'Chocksy' were working on the top Roman bit and the 'I-tie' told me the Celts were down the slope. I always gave priority to the Celts and worked there, when suddenly a range rover came tearing onto the field and stopped right beside the 'I-tie'. It turned out to be the Marcus of Blamford and two of his friends. They were having a conversation with the 'I-tie', basically telling them what they were doing. As bold as brass and without any inhibitions, we're metal detecting. So, the Marcus may have been showing off to his friends, said "have you found anything?" The 'I-tie' had about half a dozen Roman coins in his pocket and he showed them to him. He didn't have anything of value, so he gave them to Marcus, who was very pleased. Seeing this reaction, the 'I-tie' asked if it was okay if we could search this field and he said we could. We used this encounter to our advantage for years. Because even after his father had disowned him, we still maintained that we had permission. Though, things had changed.

A few years later, 'Carrottop' and I were on the site but

this time at night and we were working away on the site and at about maybe 11:30pm, we heard an enormous crash. We knew there had been an accident. The young locals used the backroads as a bit of a race course, because it ran parallel to the main road. There was a crash at the end of the road. We heard the sirens and the blue lights, but we had a pretty good idea of what had happened. Everything went quiet by about 3am and we hadn't had a particularly good night, but this was the nature of the site. Some days you would find coins, others you wouldn't. As it had been quiet for a couple of hours, we figured it had all gone, so we jumped into the car and drove towards Woodstock. Now there are no turn offs, so we drove the way we were going into a police roadblock. Because although everyone had gone, the car was still there on its side in the hedge and the police were waiting for the recovery vehicle. What we didn't know was that at the other end of the road behind us, another police car had blocked the road off, so the police were saying where the hell had you come from? So, we said oh we've come from Wood Farm. Well, we were dressed for night hawking, so we looked a bit dodgy, so the police officer said to his mate, pop down to the farm and see if that's true. So, we said oh we weren't in this farm, we were on the field near the farm. "Oh, what were you doing there?". "We were metal detecting". So, they looked round the vehicle and found the detectors in the boot and they accepted that explanation. Then it came up, "have you got permission?". "Oh yes", we said, "from Marcus'". So, we were bluffing, but we had a pretty good idea that they weren't going to bang on the door of Blenheim Palace to ask if we had permission to metal detect. The bluff worked and they let us go. We then went home.

We knew from other people that had been stopped on the site, that detecting wasn't permitted and we found out eventually first-hand. One day, 'Bootsy' and I were going to Number 10 and he had a friend who had an antique shop in Woodstock, and he had arranged to meet him there that afternoon. Well, it was more evening really, we arranged to meet him around 5:30pm. I can't remember what it was he wanted to see him for but anyway, we just made it in time, and we were in the shop when a Lord friend of mine turned up (who wants to remain anonymous). Anyway, he was a frequent visitor to Blenheim Palace, and he was going there in 2 days' time and invited me along. So, I thought this would be a good opportunity to have a word with the Duke and try and get permission. So, we turned up and there was a meeting going on about a vintage car rally. I thought the timing wasn't right to bring up the subject, so decided to desert my anonymity. So, when we left, I had a word with my friend on his next visit, to ask the Duke on my behalf. After about 2 weeks, he phoned me and told me that the archaeologists had got there before me. The archaeological department of Oxford had asked the Duke not to allow any detecting on his land, which he had agreed to and I wouldn't expect him to break his word. This of course is not the first time I've heard this. One example that comes to mind way back in the day, in my naivety, I would ask farmers for permission. I had done some research and I had found references to a Roman villa, actually what the references had said was that ruins had been found of Roman buildings; just north of Pugridge. So, I found the farm and decided to go up and ask for permission. I got there in the morning and it was harvest time. It was a pretty damp and horrible day, but I drove into the farmyard and I could see something was going on because there was a pile of grain and a grain blower in the middle of the yard. These grain blowers are designed to dry the grain off, sucking it up and blowing it into a sheltered area. and then the farmer, on a later date, would blow it again into the silo. If the grain goes into the silo damp, it will ferment and rot. So, I waited for about half an hour, when a tractor came in with a trailer behind it, reversed up and started to tip the grain onto a smaller pile already there. The guy didn't pay me too much attention, he was in a hurry, but he did ask me whether I wanted anything. But I sensed that the opportunity wasn't right. If I had just blurted it out, he probably would have just said no and sent me on my way. So, I was engaging him in general farm talk. They like that if you start asking them questions about farming. He was in a bit of a rush and that he was short-handed and that I would have to come back tomorrow if I wanted to see him about anything. This I didn't want to do. So, I said, could I help in any way? He said, "yes please, if you could?". All I needed to do was to keep an eye on the blower, so that he could go to get the next load. If the blower had blown the gain off, then he showed me how to turn it off. That is all I needed to do. He was rushing because the forecast for that night was heavy rain. Anyway, I stayed there all day and he came in and out with various loads. He bought the last load in at about 9pm and I finally got to talk to him and ask him if I could detect. There were only two I was interested in and I wanted to detect those fields. Then he hit me with a bombshell, he had signed an agreement with the Archaeological society, and he wasn't allowed to let anyone detect on his land.

This attitude seemed to be fairly strong in the south, for instance, in my area of Hertfordshire, most of the land is owned by two people, Lord Aldenham and the Borough Council. By the way, when I first knew Lord Aldenham, he lived in Aldenham, now he lives in Surrey, go figure. I know a tenant farmer of the County Council, on whose land I have an apery. Even though you can argue that that land is owned by us, you're not allowed on and certainly, no metal detecting. But the control goes further than that. There is a big wood at the top of the hill on his farm and even he is not allowed in there!

Hawking can be Dangerous

There are two occasions where things got a bit hairy. One the first occasion 'Bootsy', 'Pig' and I were going to Balon house. Now Balon house is on one side of a dual carriageway, and from our point of view, it's on the side we were travelling up which is quite handy. When they built the dual carriageway, they cut through the top of the hill, so the site runs from there downwards. Coincidently, there just happens to be a lay-by opposite the middle field. So 'Bootsy' told me to pull into the lay-by and he would run up the embankment, which from the lay-by is about nine feet and would see if the field was ready for us. So 'Pig' and I were watching him go up the embankment, having a bit of a laugh, as it was damp and he was slip-sliding everywhere. When he reached the top, he was just short of the summit, but he stretched up to peer over the top and then suddenly, he fell backwards and came tumbling down, then he ran over to the car all in a panic, shouting "fuck me, they're shooting at us!" The road was quiet, as it always is at that time of night, so I roared off. Before we left we already knew that if the fields of Balem weren't ready, we would go onto Exworth, which is where I was heading. After a minute or two, 'Bootsy' had calmed down and then realised and he said "They couldn't have been shooting at me, they couldn't have known I was there" So we concluded that they were probably after rabbits or deer. So we went to Exworth and as it happened I had a very satisfying night, as I found my best, and first heraldic broach, on which was up amongst my best finds.

On the second occasion it was 'Rat' and I; by the way 'Rat' was called 'Rat' because of his work but as it turns out 'Rat' by name, 'Rat' by nature. Anyway, we'd gone to Ashwell, but to a different area of the field previously mentioned. From this particular area, you can see right down into the valley and left and right. As we were working in the far distance, we could see an infrared lamp being used by someone hunting. They used these infrared lights because it doesn't spook the game and it also enables you to use night scopes. Anyway, they were a long way off, two or three fields over. 'Rat' was a bit worried, but I reassured him, it wouldn't be the farmer, it would be someone he had sold the shooting rights to, and that he should ignore it and carry on, which we did. But detecting is carried out just using the sound, which means you can keep your eye on what's going on around you. So with one eye on this red lamp waving all over the place, we carried on. After about fifthteen or twenty minutes, the light had moved across and was now on the same bridal way that we were next to, but still a long way off. Then we suddenly heard the cracking of bullets over our head as Bootsy had experienced at Balon. We both hit the deck and lay there for a few minutes, there were one or two more cracks and then I noticed the light had moved off and was now out of sight. So although what they were doing under British shooting law, is hardly legal, to the finer details of which I won't go into, they didn't seem to be bothered, but as the light was no longer in sight, we carried on. After about fifthteen minutes, suddenly quite close on the track way, the truck appeared and the inferred light was turned straight onto us, first onto 'Rat' and then onto me. They weren't doing anything, they were just standing there with the light on us watching us work. I said to 'Rat' ``ignore them, just start working your way towards the car" which was at a forty-five degree angle across the field. They turned the red light out and drove very slowly along the track until they were beside us, we carried on and they drove slowly down the field to the road. They crossed the road and picked up the track on the other side, but the far end of that track there is a farm about half a mile away. They were moving slowly down the track and although we could see their brake lights going on and off, I knew they could not see us. So we walked briskly to the car and it was a case of who reached the finish line first, when we reached the car we didn't bother to change, we just jumped in it and drove off. Better to be on the safe side and just leave.

Heavly Clipped Late Roman Silver Siliqua

5

Doing Somebody an Involuntary Favour

One night as all these escapades started, 'Little shit', the others and I decided to go to Walsingham. For a change we went in Gazza's car, as we usually went in mine. Gazza has one of those small Volvo hatchback things, or a shit box in other words. We reached the town, reckied the small roads that surrounded the site but 'shit's' sixth sense was ringing alarm bells and he felt it was uneasy, so the group decided not to go to the main Roman site.

Now 'Little shit' and 'Gazza' knew of a mediaeval site that I was unaware of, which was on the hill at the other side of town, about a mile away. We parked the car about half way along an overgrown farm track way and proceeded onto the field and started to metal detect. From the fields that we were on, we had a commanding view of the main road below us. We started at the far end of the field, but this was not a good idea as it was relatively early. Instead we had to stay there as the other end of the field was housing.

After about an hour we saw a police car coming along the road moving away from the town. There was a sharp left-hand bend which the police car started to go around but then suddenly stopped. It then reversed into the gateway to face back to the way it had come from and then turned off all of its lights.

We were not sure what this Babylon was doing but we didn't feel any danger, so we carried on detecting. A further half an hour passed when we suddenly saw the sky light up, and the sun came out. We realised that they were flares and we knew from the position of these that some poor bastard was getting the run-around on the Roman site; though we did find this funny.

Then our friend, 'the plod' turned on his lights, started up and rolled into town. By this time, I had hooked up with 'Gazza' by the hedge and we were having a smoke and a chat. I said to 'Gazza' we should be alright because they're after them. Then we heard the dim sound of engines revving in the background, but we didn't care, we just carried on. A further 10 minutes later the Babylon car returned and parked in the same spot, facing town with its lights off. We regrouped in the field by the hedge again and I said they couldn't have caught them as they were still chasing them around. After further discussion it was decided that once the police car had moved on, we were out here because the car was blocking us in. We then slowly and casually made our way back to our car watching 'the plod' at all times.

Once we had reached the car and put the machines in the boot and so on, we heard the police car roar off again. Still no urgency but as a precaution I told 'Gazza' to leave his lights off, which he then proceeded to do.

The track we were on was terrible, full of potholes and ruts and loads of vegetation. About 50 yards away we could see the headlights of another Babylon car bobbing up and down because of the ditches. At this point, I believe he still hadn't seen us but was busy looking for the other crew they were originally chasing.

'Gazza', who was now under the adrenaline of panic, turned on his lights and dropped the hammer. The car then accelerated down this track And drew the attention of the unaware Babylon car that was now giving us chase with blue flashing lights. It was clear they were after us.

We'd reached the main road and turned right and left town. I looked out the back of the window to see yet another Babylon car heading towards us with blue flashing lights, thereby making two in total. I said to 'Gazza', "go for it, Gaz" but there was no need as he was already belting up the road.

We were steaming up and around those narrow Norfolk lanes putting a bit of distance between us and the two old bill, but bit by bit they were cutting into our already slim lead. If we had kept going straight on the road that we were on it was inevitable that Babylon would catch us by using a roadblock or by simply catching up to us. Me being Billy Brain Box, I came up with the idea to switch off all the lights and turn left or right at the first opportunity this would mean leaving the lights off two or 3 miles after we've made the turn. Here we could then bring the speed down to about 30 mph.

Fortunately, we have the walking roadmap in the car with 'Little shit' navigating, which was good as he knew the area like the back of his hand. They seemed to work the first time as we saw the police car go past the end of the road. Once Gazzer felt confident, he then switched on his lights and went back to full speed going as fast as he could in his Volvo. As I was riding shotgun, I looked out the back for any bad guys.

I think turning the lights back on was a bit premature as I hadn't seen the other car pass the end of the road, so the old turn the lights off and run ploy seemed to have worked. Suddenly out of nowhere, I was looking out of the window, we had a Babylon car looking large up our arse. 'Gazza', who was panicking, switched into his Collin MacCray Mode and lived out his fantasy of being a rally driver. Though as we were in Volvo, he threw the car from left to right and rattled us around like three marbles in a tin. I'll give 'Gazza' what he's due, as it was a wild ride, but he did slowly manage to pull away from the pursuer; far enough in fact that we could repeat the same process again. This time it worked and we were able to travel about 13 miles without going through a town, that's how good 'Little shit's' knowledge was of the area. From experience we knew if we'd gone through the town, roadblocks would have been set up and we would've been caught. After all, whoever the police were chasing originally had got away from the Roman site at our expense, given that they were too busy chasing us to chase them. If any of you guys read this book, we were the crew who were being chased that night. You owe us one boys!

The Americans

Over the years, 'Old Boy' had organised detecting trips for Americans in England. It has worked out quite well. He didn't take them on really hot sites, most of them that is, but there was a handful who came back year after year; which we got to know well, and they wanted to go on the hot sites.

To this day, he still organises trips and brings them over. There was only one incident I can remember where they nearly got caught and it was more luck than judgement that they didn't. We were all down on Mildenhall and we had had a successful night. From there, the run back to Norfolk was quite a run. So, they were leaving early, at about 2 am. Oldboy walked to one end with the Americans and stood by the gate and sent 'Gazza' to go and get the car. Now they had parked the car in a silly place. They parked outside a school nearby, which we would never have done, as it draws attention to you. At the end of the field where 'Gazza' was, there was a small lane that cuts between the two fields. The lane is down lower than the field. So, it's quite steep down to the road. So, Gazza pushed his way through the hedge and gave his machine to 'Old Boy' and him and the Americans walked across to the other end. So, 'Gazza' had got through the hedge but was unable to stop himself sliding on the wet grass to the road. Straight in front was an unmarked police car. Apparently, the next day, there was supposed to be some Royal visit in the area, and they were just patrolling. So, they marched him back to the car, which was in 'Old Boy''s name, I don't know what excuse he gave but he didn't admit to metal detecting. But the paperwork on the car didn't match up, so they ceased the car and took 'Gazza' in. They released him the next morning, but left 'Old Boy' and the Americans stranded. We got them back by cramming everybody into different cars. 'Old Boy' couldn't admit to the car being his and so, never got it back. But 'Gazza' wasn't arrested and walked free. He was then stranded down there but he telephoned a friend who drove down there and picked him up.

Nice Roman Ant Coin

6

On an Island with Nowhere to Run

On one of the many excursions to Walsingham, a new guy, 'Old Boy', myself and two other guys (who had never been metal detecting before, met up at 'Old Boy's' house.

'Carrottop' and 'Bootsy' were also supposed to have arrived but by 11:30pm, we received a phone call from 'Bootsy' who appeared to be pissed as a parrot. He went on to say that 'Carrottop' was also pissed out of his head, meaning he didn't know his name nor where he lived. The four of us then decided to go to Walsingham for a session there.

We arrived and got to the site without any hassle and started work on the bank field, which was away from the road towards one of the rivers situated around the site. After an hour or so had passed, we heard a car with the lights turned off stop at the end of the field. Even at this point we knew the night was over and again had finished. We then grouped up and watched how things would unfold.

Torches had now been switched on and they had fanned out across the field, heading towards us. This was the signal to switch into high gear and leg it. The plan was to take off towards the edge of the wood in the knowledge that there is a single plank footbridge across both streams. This escape route means you have to cross two bridges before you cross the very tip of an island surrounded by water. This is not a problem as I had my Wellies on. We proceeded to cross the first bridge in single file, with 'Old Boy' going first, swiftly followed by myself and then the two others.

The gap between the bridges stood for about 40 feet so we proceeded in single file onto the second bridge. At the end of that bridge, there was a cow field and a sty. 'Old Boy' was already on the sty making his way over and we waited our turns.

Straight across from the sty on the other side of the field is a road which we were heading for when out of thin air a police car came roaring down the road and stopped. The police car had overshot a gap in the hedge that we were heading for. At this point I thought "there's a result, you missed it", as they missed it by 60 yards or so. This meant that when they got their searchlights out, they lit the field in the wrong place. We could then see more lights coming over the brow of the field at the exit, which was now cut-off. We all had faces like clockwork soldiers and started to head back towards the first bridge in robot fashion. You must understand that this bridge was bloody small. 'Old Boy' was now bringing up the gear and supported what appeared to be a pathway going into the trees. Saying "this way chaps", we went like lambs to a kebabs shop and followed 'Old Boy' who led us down the 30 foot track.

At the end of this path was a small thick undergrowth but once 'Old Boy' crashed through it, he made enough noise to wake up an entire community of dead people in Glasgow. We continue to pretend to be Dr Livingstone, hacking our way through this jungle-like terrain but we were not getting anywhere. After I had fallen over a fallen log which 'Old Boy' had gotten over easily. I was then stung by some stinging nettles, which felt like they were trying to eat me. In actual fact I'm still moaning about this to the very day as I'm a miserable git and it pees me off.

Once 'Old Boy' and the others had stopped laughing, I called 'Old Boy' over to my battered body and discussed our escape plan. 'Old Boy' and I both needed to stay well with the other two as they had no idea where they were and were just following us. It dawned on me where we were and I said to 'Old Boy', "aren't we on the island?" He replied, "well yeah." I snapped back, saying "we better get off here, how's your breaststroke?"

Turning around we headed back towards the bridges not forgetting to throw some abuse into the log and the man eating nettles. We made our way towards bridge number two which was in the direction of the police car and the lone plod. We got over the sty and turned left. At this point I looked back behind me to see the police car had moved from its original spot only to stop by the gateway of the field. You could see it was a Land Rover at this point, as he was standing in his headlights trying to open the gate. We ran at top speed along the river embankment parallel with the island and across the field at an angle.

I knew if the policemen had got into the field, he was going to be doing some off-roading, as he had no intention of running around a muddy field in his clean boots. By the time we had reached the end of the island, we did a 45° turn through the field to the road. We then all heaped up in the roadside ditch and waited until the coast was clear before running across. To our good fortune, he didn't see us and drove on by. As soon as his tailgate vanished from the view, we were up and across that road crashing through the hedge onto the field behind. We felt safe and protected as we were stranded in a field of ripe, uncut corn. We didn't stop and made it through the corner until we reached the top of the hill, where we then put our tools down and had a smoke.

From this vantage point we could see the chaos below us, Babylon cars were buzzing around like angry Scalextric cars. Men in fields with torches were all looking for us but little did they know, we were looking at them. The panic was on and off, but the only thing we had to do was make it back to the car and quietly slip into the night and make our escape yet again. In hindsight we were lucky on this occasion that they didn't use flares; it was great to know the local yokels have got sophisticated and have joined the 21st century.

Don't Let Fame go to Your Head

I would just like to mention that on two occasions, our gang had been on Channel 5. The first instance was with 'Bootsy', 'Pig' and 'Gazza'. They were approached by Channel 5 to do a documentary on Knight Hawking. They were gonna be paid £160 each and 'Bootsy' invited me. I said no because as far as I could see, this was a double edged sword. But they were all about earning money and decided to go ahead with it. So, the three of them went off to a Roman site called Great Chesterfield, with the film crew and low light cameras. They picked that particular site knowing full well they would get a chase, which was the whole point of the program and sure enough, they got chased off. Everybody escaped and the film crew were happy, and it went out on air. But the week after it went out on air, 'Pig' walked into the dole office to find they had suspended his benefits because he had been recognised by a member of staff and he hadn't declared his earnings. He was quite upset about that and then about a month later, 'Bootsy' was caught on Baylem House and he had been brought down by a spectacular rugby tackle by all accounts by an officer who back at the police station recognised him from the program and this had a reverse effect. Because of that, they let him go.

The second occasion was just Gazza. He had been approached by some Americans who wanted to do a Channel 5 program on a famous lost Roman hoard. This was not so much a hoard but instead was a huge payroll going through Romania. The Americans needed a gang of Englishmen who happened to be known by Channel 5 in order to get them to fund it. Which they did. On the back of which, an American company gave them all new metal detectors, as they were going to be shown on film. So, they all went off to Romania. When they got to Romania and they met up with the archaeologist involved, they weren't allowed to search where they wanted to search and it turned out to be a con by the Americans. What they were actually doing was looking at old castles and fortified houses with a view on doing Dracula tours. So, they were more interested in building up a portfolio but there wasn't anything Gazza could do about it and they just stayed the two weeks, did a little bit of Knight Hawking while they were out there but were restricted in their movements, so bided their time and came home.

Here's a verse from me for your amusement,
Now we are half way through,
Time for a break, time for a brew,
So put the kettle on and we will have some tea,
Whilst you read a verse from me,

Twilight falls all around,
Turning to night as we hit the sight,
That we will search to dawn,
Searching for that allusive gold,
That we would adorn,
So have a go and you may see,
The joy and ecstasy,
Of holding antiquity,

Ciao Bambino

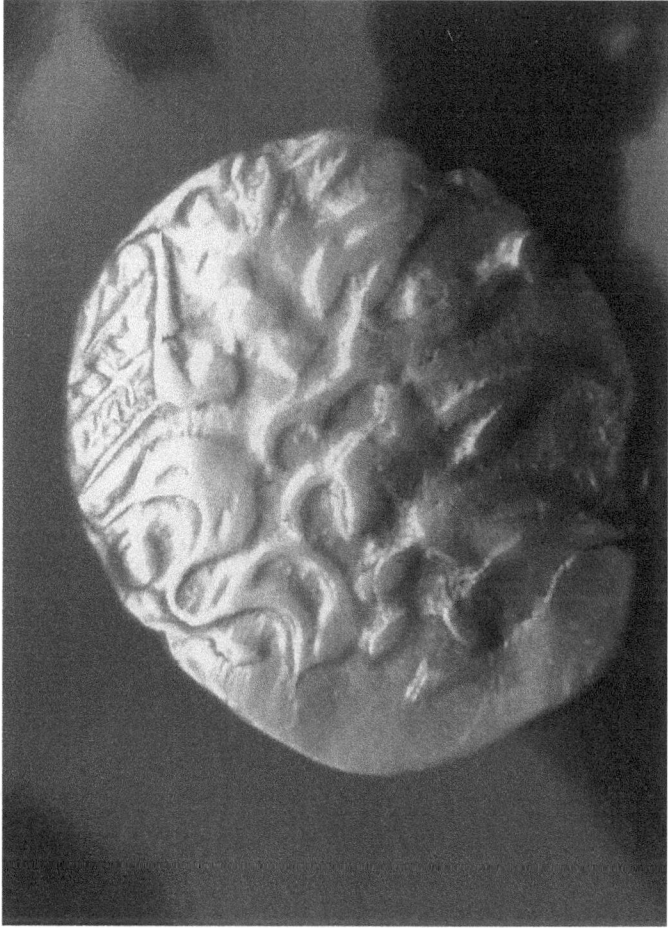

Quarter Stator Celtic Obverse

7

Frontal Lobotomy

The meeting place in that particular era was 'Old Boy's' house and, on this night, there were about 12 of us, including a guy known as 'Brain Dead' or 'LB' (Frontal Lobotomy) for short, was also there that night.

LB was a rather stupid guy and had previously made several mistakes. For example, we had gone to a site called Stonea looking for Celtic coins. This was a site that was very hard to get onto, as it had a nasty bridge over a massive dyke and obstacles to get over, around and under. This was the type of place you didn't want to get a run. Once finally on the field with our machines swinging, all of us worked away and after an hour saw 'LB' coming across the field like a cannonball shouting "run." None of us had any idea who we were running from. We made it to the other side of the field and were all displeased with LB who was unsure of what he had done. As it turned out, he thought he saw a light but due to his mistake, we sent him back to Coventry and continued to have a good night.

On another instance, 'Old Boy' decided he was not

going out, so I went to the site by myself. As it was dusk it was still early, and I decided to strong it out a bit and take a risk. I worked about half way across the field towards the hotspot when I saw the headlights of the vehicle driving round the hedge of the grass field opposite. I knew the angle I was at meant they couldn't see what I was doing but after hearing a shotgun go off, I realised they were rabbiting. They were plotted upin the corner of the field and every 45 minutes or so they would roar around the field blowing big holes in little rabbits. I carried on in the knowledge that they wouldn't come to the ploughed field and quietly worked across the hotspot. I then noticed seven or eight guys making their way over to me. I could make out they were fellow hawkers but didn't want them to realise that I was on my hotspot, so I pretended I was just travelling through and going somewhere else on the site.

This crew hadn't searched their way over, they just B lined for me as one or two of them recognised me from an earlier account and wanted to chat. To my absolute dismay they switched on and started to work my zone, my hotspot. I knew that one of them had found coins and they were going to be there for the night. They spread out in a line in front of me and worked the area I was about to do. This just pissed me off more. After that a great Celt in the sky came to my aid from the farmer. The farmer was now on the move again with his shot gun in hand and after firing, the hawkers ran past me like Road Runner. All that was missing was the classic "Meep, Meep." These guys did not stop until they reached the edge of the field, but I remained calm and collected and carried on swinging my stick without a care in the world. However, the crew made their way back to me again once they realised what the farmer was doing. By this time, they reached me, but I'd cunningly moved away from my hotspot and is now a new area. One of the guys came up to me and said, "didn't you run?" I simply replied, "no, they were only rabbiting.

I continued to search for about another hour and no booty was found. Though I did already have four silver units in my pocket anyway and it was about 11 in evening with the two hour drive to get home, so I thought sod it, I'm off and I left.

An Accidental Find

One night, 'I-tie' and 'Carrottop' and I went to the Roman site of Bletchley. We'd only just got onto the field and I walked across to one of the corners which I knew had a few coins. The other two stood directly opposite the gate when a police car pulled into the gateway, headlights lighting them up. So, I ran under the hedge and where I was, they couldn't see me. The other two ran down the field, keeping as close to the hedge as possible. I hid my machine under the hedge and just walked down the road to where we were parked, which was a Little Chef car park. So, they ran down the field to another gateway, crossed over the road and came back up the field on the other side, so were now behind the police. It was a very thick hedge, so they knew they were okay. I had gone to the top of the field where there was another gateway and looked over and I could see them standing there looking over and trying to see through it. By now, the Babylon had gone but were driving round and round. I went into the field and walked over to them and they were searing the field. It was perfect for working and they were metal detecting it. By the time I had got to them, they had found a couple of Denarii each. They showed me they had found roman coins in this field, which we didn't normally search. So, I ran back to where I had hidden my metal detector and then came back, and we carried on searching to find more Denarii. This turned out to be a scattered hoard. We found this accidentally. We took all of the coins to a dealer we knew, who analysed them and going by the different emperors and the range, concluded that this would have been a very big hoard. This was just a lucky find.

A Random Thought

I would just like to say a word about the thrill of metal detecting, at least for me. When you find for the first time, an ancient coin or artefact, it's very exciting because you hold the piece and you know that it's Roman. You know it's been in the ground for at least 1500 years. When you're the first person to touch that, and in my case, it was definitely a Roman coin, it was what we call Shot Roman coin; which means it was very badly worn and unidentifiable, with just a few bumps. The fact that it's bronze as well also gives away that it's Roman. That particular coin is what is known as an A4. Although these were of very little value, when you find a denarius or a siliqua, the value increases. So, this conjures up all sorts of thoughts. What effect did this have on the person who lost it? - As in today, if you lost a £50 note, how would that affect you? Would that mean going without a meal or something? So, finding these coins gets you wondering about the effects on that person. The same goes for broaches; these had numerous functions and were valuable to those who owned them. Holding garments together etc. So, I can't emphasise enough the thrill of holding that thing for the first time and after all these years, that feeling still hasn't gone away. and when that feeling goes, it's time to hang up your detector.

Quarter Stator Celting Reverse

8

Oblivious

One night there was 'Oblivious', 'Two phones' and I on our way to a site known as the Cliff. En route, you have to pass a RAF Scampton the home of the 617 Squadron or The Dam Busters. On the outside perimeter of the airfield is a Roman villa, the field had just been flattened off and perfect for detecting. We parked up in a little car park that was higher than the field and overlooked it. We then realised this was just a shagger's carpark. We all turned on our machines and off we went. 'Two phones' was working close to me and 'Oblivious' was in his own world with headphones in his ears. He was completely oblivious to anything, hence his nickname, 'Oblivious'.

After finding a few coins, 'Oblivious' went off on his own and had gone up a large bank, as our current spot was in the middle of the valley. You must remember this is an active RAF base, so security was high. Tension was also high between the British government and certain members of the Irish community, which was not great. I was on full alert watching out for Babylon and worst of all military Babylon.

It was also pitch black so the light showed up for miles when you were in the car park.

A very powerful Spotlight then came from the car park and started panning over the field. We charged across the field in order to make it to the edge where there was a thick hedge. This hedge was so thick we could easily hide in it, all for except 'Oblivious' who had gone off elsewhere. 'Oblivious' was still unaware of this point. There was a car which turned out to be local Babylon who had obviously seen my car in the park and stopped to check it. Upon checking it they found no one in it and decided to look for where we were.

The coppers were standing by the car when another car arrived and these two were having a chat just as a third car pulled in. We all felt our ring pieces start to twitch and were getting ready to run. We needed a cunning plan, as the Babylon were scanning over the field quickly. We made our way through the hedge to the surrounding field and hid by the hedge on the other side. We felt safe in the corn as it was a perfect hiding spot, but we knew 'Oblivious' was still being scoped.

All three of us popped our heads over the hedge every now and again and could see 'Oblivious' in the distance being caught very dimly in the beam of the light. We had a rough idea of where he was and the Babylon didn't. After a while the Babylon must've gotten bored as they turned off the lights and pulled out of the car park. At this point, we stayed for a while and had an obligatorily smoke and discussed whether we should have gone to get 'Oblivious'. I turned to 'Two phones' and said, "walk up the hedge and get the car", to which he responded with "Fuck you!".

After a bit of professional heckling from 'Paddy' and I, 'Two phones' agreed to go and get the car and bring it up to where 'Oblivious' was. 'Two phones' being six foot four and heavily built, stuck out anywhere. We decided that him walking down the dark road ahead with his shoulders above the hedge was a stupid idea but he went anyway in his hawker uniform to collect the vehicle. 'Paddy' and I saw the lights come on and heard the engine start. 'Two phones' then came flying out of nowhere and 'Paddy' and I disrobed quickly, throwing everything into the boot. 'Oblivious' was still nowhere to be seen.

With 'Two phones' in the driver's seat and me in the passenger seat, 'Paddy' was refusing to get in the car while trying to get 'Oblivious'' attention. Signalling across the field with a pocket torch, 'Two phones' started to become very pissed off and wanted to leave but knew he couldn't without 'Oblivious'. That being said, we also knew we had to leave as the plod would soon be back.

At this point, tempers started to fray, as precious time ticked away. 'Oblivious' then walked through the gate saying, "where are you lot going?" He was completely oblivious to the whole escapade and didn't even know about us running to the adjacent field. 'Oblivious' then got in the car still robed and 'Two phones' sped off as quickly as possible. This was another close shave but no cigar.

Another episode with 'Oblivious' is when we all went on the Arc. I had been given the night off from driving on this occasion, which was a welcomed change, so 'Paddy' and I went in 'Oblivious'' Ford Transit pick up.

When we reached the site, 'Oblivious' parked nose first in the gateway to a field on the opposite side of the road.

The entrance to the field we wanted to search is directly opposite the gateway we had parked in but in our field, there was no gate.

We crossed the first field and went to the far side of the site, which is the second field behind the public house (The Arc).

I personally don't like this site very much, as you tend to only get a lot of small bronze Roman coins, most of which are shot. By that I mean they have been rubbed smooth, so there is no head or writing on them. Although, on a previous occasion, 'Paddy' did find a nice, gold Roman Ring off there.

Well, I had been on that little area for some two hours and by now boredom was setting in. We had all split up but as per usual, 'Oblivious' had gone off in his own little world. I started to look for 'Paddy' but unbeknown to me, he had already moved into the field first. I made my way through the hedge there and went into the first field looking for 'Paddy' as part of this particular field is lit up by streetlights, so it makes it easier to spot someone.

I lurked with intent by the hedge for a while, having the compulsory fag surveying the field looking for 'Paddy'. From where I was, I could see 'Oblivious" truck and the tailgate was facing me. In the shadows, I could see what looked like movement and what appeared to be the interior light, which was on.

Knowing that 'Paddy' felt about the site the same way as I did, my first thought was that those bastards are getting ready to do the off and hadn't told me. "Slags" I said to myself and made my way towards the truck. Partly as a precaution and partly a habit, I didn't b-line for the gateway but headed for the hedge some 50 yards down from where the truck was parked.

The field slopes down towards the road and by being by the hedge at the end of the field, I had lost the advantage of being on high ground. I couldn't see over the hedge, so I walked down its length and got about 20 or 30 feet from the gate when I froze on the spot.

A Babylon had stepped through the gateway and is now on the field. "What do I do?" He had the biggest torch a man could carry and was illuminating the field with it. I crouched down by the hedge and prayed he didn't turn up and light me up. I couldn't run as he would have heard me and would have captured me, so I put in an emergency call to God and asked if he could help me out.

The Babylon then shone his torch round and round the field like he was pretending to be a lighthouse, and this seemed to go on forever. He then switched off his torch if you can call it that and stepped back onto the road.

Staying in a crouched position, I started to walk the hedge again without breaking into a run until I figured I must have been out of ear shot and had put some distance between me and the Babylon. Once I figured out I was relatively safe, that was it, full revs, like scalded cats and ran up the other hedgerow, which took me back to where I had a smoke.

Once there, I could see movement around the truck, but my view was poor, so I manoeuvred to get a better angle of sight on the gateway. I kept going up the hedge line to get a better view and could see silhouettes of people and lights all around the truck; which was our means of escape. At one point, I could see a plod standing on the back of the pick-up shining a torch into the cab.

I slowly worked my way up the hedge line gaining height as I went. A little way from my location stands a pylon, inside the pylon the grass always grows long, as you can't plough inside the legs of a pylon.

Standing there still watching the trick, I was aware of somebody running towards me from the pylon, it was that area that the Babylon had been centring their search on. I was on the verge of running when I could see whoever was running, was running in a crouched position. This person turned out to be 'Paddy' fortunately.

'Paddy' and I stood in the hedge row, obliged to have another fag and 'Paddy' bitched about the fact that I am smoking, as it gave us a good chance of being caught, given the glowing cherry on the end of my fag. This wasn't going to happen though, as I was an old hand at this game and knew how to hide my glowing orange cigarette.

'Paddy' told me he had been working the pylon area, which ain't a bad spot to search actually but had seen the whole thing unfold, police arriving, searching the field with spotlights, the lot. All 'Paddy' did was to enter the pylon and lay down in the grass because it had not been cut. Eventually, the first Babylon car left but unbeknown to me, there was still another one parked up down the road, and we couldn't see it, but 'Paddy' knew it was there. Somewhere anyway.

'Paddy' said hang on, so I lit up another fag, as you do, fifteen minutes passed and then the second Babylon left. It was time to make our escape. Yep, you guessed it, where the fuck was 'Oblivious'.

We went back through the hedge into the second field to look for 'Oblivious' and had got about half way down the field and there he was swinging the stick. We approached him at some speed with the message let's fuck off, 'Oblivious' replied "why, we aren't going now are we?" oblivious was completely and utterly oblivious to all that had happened with the police and them being on, over and under his truck and also the fact the first police car shot off up the road with blue lights flashing.

What planet is he on and what planet does he come from? Another evening bolloxed and all to show for it was a handful of shots aways. The saving grace in all of this was that 'Oblivious' could no longer go out hawking, as he had a work-related injury to his back. We would miss him if we could find him.

Roman Broach

9

Holes and Digs

In the summer months, metal detecting goes out of the window because crops are growing and our type of metal detecting means that it's not possible. It's true you can still search on grass fields and on some market garden sites, but we tend not to do that. Although, with the modern machines the grass sites are now beginning to look more possible. And in this country, I just don't like working the beaches. So the other forms of treasure hunting is digging holes. Although 'Carrottop' didn't introduce me to this activity, we did do a few together. The first one being a site called Wombra. Wombra is a well known Celtic shrine and votive site, so on this site the coins found are predominantly Minums and they are bronze, which is quite nice, and silver. But the silver being of very low grade, makes them difficult to find. So, the technique we devised was one person would dig and put the earth to one side, while the other with the detector would flatten the soil down and make it as thin as possible. They would then go over and over slowly because the minums are very easy to miss. So, quite slow going.

When you got down to the clay, you would then stamp it out to make it as thin as possible. And go all metal!

The site was adjacent to a very well-worn footpath which goes back to ancient times, so if you walked along, literally on the other side of the fence, was the site. So normally this would be carried out at night but on this occasion in winter, we arrived about 11 o'clock mid-week. The weather was inclement and we figured this would put a lot of dog walkers off, so we took a chance. We had been working 2 or 3 hours and everything was going lovely. We had 3 silver and 1 bronze and the odd dog walker that came past, we just hid behind the hedge and let them pass. Now from the site, if you look across the site at a 45 degree angle, you could clearly see the farm house and all was going well until dusk started to fall.

'Carrottop' was down the hole, so he couldn't see much but me standing up, I was also acting as a watch out apart from a searcher. I started seeing lights coming on and off in the farmhouse which was okay until I saw an upstairs light come on, for about 5 minutes and then went off. But we carried on, nothing to worry about we thought and then suddenly, the outside security light came on. Now this caught our attention but we didn't panic but cautiously we carried on. Then the security light went out but then I could see somebody with a torch waving it around and it looked like they may be coming towards us. Although we didn't feel there was any danger, we were happy with what we had found, I said to 'Carrottop', "that'll do" and off we went.

So on the next occasion, we went to Barking to dig the river bank. Back then it was quite easy to get to, as you could go down the stairs during low tide and then you simply dug down. Whilst 'Carrottop' was getting started, I walked the foreshore and picked up as many clay pipes as I could and just generally had a look round. This site was not hot in any way at all, so we just carried on until the tide turned and we could no longer carry on. We found a few Victorian and Georgian coins, nothing really of any value and it quite an uneventful dig.

On our next trip, we went to Cambridge. so what they do in Cambridge, not every summer but some summers, they divert the river around the town which lowers the water flow right down to almost nothing. The reason for this is they would then repair the walls either side all along throughout the town. So, if you dig, you can only do this on the weekend when the maintenance crews aren't working. But 'Carrottop' had heard from someone else that this had happened, so we arrived, looking for a spot to get down onto the foreshore. The only way we found was by cutting across campus, so no public, and we dropped down under a very old accommodation block and we proceeded in our own time, as we didn't have to worry about the tide. This turned out to be a very poor dig as we did not find any coins to my disappointment, as I'm only there for the coins. But we did find a few silver spoons. Now some silver spoons if they go back far enough, are quite valuable and two of them were, which we sold to a dealer friend. The other thing we found is a weird bronze implement, which to this day, I have never found anybody that has any idea of what it is. Not even the museums. So, after a pretty hard day, we simply gave up and went home.

Next occasion, we went down to Farley Heath. Farley Heath is the site of a Celtic temple; all that's actually there now are some concrete walls at ground level, which the archeologists have installed just to show the site. There was also a signboard in the front explaining what we were looking at. It comprised of an outer wall in a square, with an inner wall in a square and then a solid square in the middle. The ground work around this whole area is very very sandy, so this is also a bit of a beauty spot. Once again there were a lot of dog walkers but at least you could park on the site. When you come into the carpark, the temple is on the right hand side, just on the end of where the bracken starts. As you come in, straight in front of you to the far end, the woods, consisting of birch, start. Most dog walkers park their cars and head for that area, well away from us; even though a footpath does run down the right hand side of the temple. But if you go behind the temple, you can pull the brake to one side as the roots don't hold. so, you can clear quite a nice square, which enables you to dig.

Now on this site, you do not need a detector. It's all done with shovels and civ, so most people coming into the car park don't see you; if you keep down low, you can stay hidden amongst the bracken, which is very handy. The only thing you had to be careful of was noise. So, one person digs and puts the sandy soil into a civ and the other person just civs it. There's very few stones, so a part from the odd piece of root, it clears the civ quite quickly. So, we had been going for about 2 hours and we had one Quarter Stator when a panda car pulled into the car park. We just ducked down and kept still. He stayed for about 15 minutes and then left. We carried on for about another hour and we'd just found the second coin, quarter stator, when the panda car reappeared. By now, it was just on dusk, so at first we froze and laid in the hole, as there was no way anyone could see us. We kept quiet. But this time, after about 10 minutes, he got out of the car alone and was just generally looking around, not moving. So, we kept still. Then, a second car, a squad car, came in and pulled up alongside him. There were 4 in this car, so we knew it was something serious. So, straight away we started to crawl through the bracken but we had to cross the footpath I previously mentioned to get into a small copse of birch, so we hesitated on the edge of the footpath and waited to see what the police were doing. They made no attempt to come towards the shrine, they all got out and started to walk towards the far end. Why they didn't just drive over there, I just don't know. This was good news for us, as we allowed them to get halfway across the clearing and then we got into the copse and worked our way back round behind them. We were parked nearer to the road than the police cars were, so we were able to get into the car without them seeing or hearing us, because by now they were right across the other side of the clearing and I just simply started up, reversed and then drove out slowly; so as not to cause attention to ourselves. As far as they were concerned, we could have just been dog walkers. So, close but no cigar. Then we went home laughing our heads off.

So finally, 'Carrottop' told me that he had heard from 'LB', that he knew of a good spot at wombra to dig. I was a bit hesitant given that we were talking about LB but 'Carrottop' convinced me it would be okay. Because 'LB' lives in Norfolk, we agreed to meet in the parking areas at Wombra, which we did all fine. But this time it was at night when we arrived, and everything was going fine. He showed us the spot that he had picked out and it looked good. So, because we were an odd number, we came to an agreement whereby 'Carrottop' would dig and he would put one shovel full for 'LB' and one shovel full for us alternatively. 'LB' would keep what he found and 'Carrottop' and I would keep what I found. So, we dug for quite a few uneventful hours, a couple of dog walkers had gone by but we simply hid as we usually do. I think LB had four coins and we had five but he had the better coins, that's just the way it goes. I was standing nearer the footpath than LB or 'Carrottop', who was in the hole. He couldn't see anything again as usual. So, it was about 3 o'clock and you could clearly hear any noise made around us. Me being nearest to the footpath was standing closest to the way in. At this point, I need to explain the site in more detail. This footpath starts at the end of a road but narrows down quite fast to a footpath. On the left hand side is the site but on the right hand side, opposite and level with the site, is a very dense wood. At night, you can't see more than a foot in front of yourself. So, you wouldn't want to be running into that wood. The footpath continues on for about half a mile before it breaks out into another road. so, the only real way out is the way you come in, without being trapped. Getting back, I heard the sound of tires on gravel, but I knew a vehicle could not come all the way down. So, I stepped as close as I could to the footpath and looked up the path and I could see a sneaky Babylon car coming down all lights off but I could make out the lights on the roof. So, I said as quietly but as loud as I could, "it's the Babylon, let's run." Now LB was off like a shot but he ran straight into the dreaded wood and we could hear him crashing around. 'Carrottop' and I ran into the wood but at the very edge of the wood to the adjacent field. So we had a little bit of ambient light to help us through. As we were working our way along the edge, we went 50 or 70 yards, we then jumped the fence into the field and carried on running along the edge of the wood. But we could still hear the hell of a commotion from LB. We would've been in that wood at night, so we knew it was impossible to get through unless you charged and hoped for the best. But 'Carrottop' and I worked our way as far as we could and doubled backed on ourselves, so that we could get behind the Babylon. which we did successfully and we jumped in the car and without causing too much attention, bearing in the mind the time of night, we got away as fast as we possibly could.

The following day, I telephoned LB to see what had happened. No answer. So, I phoned again in the evening; still no answer. I phoned again the following morning and then around one o'clock in the afternoon, he answered. I asked him what the hell had happened and why it has taken him so long? He said, "because I was in hospital." So, of course, I asked why and he told me that he ran into the wood as far as he could until he tripped over and fell down. The Babylon had sent two dogs in but because of the noise he was making, the dogs went for him and not 'Carrottop' and myself. The dogs had pinned him down and he couldn't move and despite calling to the police officers to call them off, they didn't. We can only assume that they thought there were three of us in there, not just one, but they would not enter the wood until dawn before they finally called the dogs off. So, then they took LB to the hospital where he then had seven stitches from dog bites. However, they did not charge him, they figured he had suffered enough and maybe they thought, he might sue, so they let him go. So, that was the end of that saga.

Now I'd like to talk about dogs. It seems very coincidental that every incidence regarding dogs involves 'Carrottop'! That is of course, unless you're talking from his point of view. He could say that every incidence involves me. So, it reminds me of the time we went down to Cirencester. Cirencester is a Roman settlement which is one of the best settlements I've seen in this country because the wall going around it is still there. So, there's lots of places to park for the tourists but in one of the corners, there's a church with a small car park. Now this is on a bend and is on a dip in the road. So, if you're coming from the right way, for instance if you're a farmer or police car, your headlights would light up the car park. Except there is space in one of the corners, for one car, which is hidden and we knew this. We never actually searched within the walls because when they excavated the site in the 30s – I've seen the photographs – the remains are 15 foot down. So, we did all the fields on the outside, all the way around. The particular site we're talking about is the better side, as there are a number of Celtic sites on this side as well. On this occasion, we parked in our usual spot, then we had to walk out of the car park, turn left and go up the hill. This was not very far because on the opposite side of the road, on the right hand side, there is a hole in the hedge, which has been made by various people. Now this leads you into the lower end of a field, so the moment you go through the hedge, you can turn on your machine and work your way up the hill searching. However, on the other side of the road, there are some cottages, so you have to be mindful of the noise.

Anyway, on previous visits, I had found the route of going through the hedge, turning right and going down the hill to the bottom of the field, where I had found nice Roman coins in the past. So, this is what I did and for some reason, and I don't know why, 'Carrottop' was dragging behind. I had seen a couple of cars come up behind, so I figured he had jumped into the hedge and waited for them to go. By the time he came through the hedge, I could see him silhouetted by the night sky. I was already at the bottom searching. I saw him working slowly up but didn't take too much notice as I was searching myself. Then suddenly, I heard him shouting and screaming, waving his metal detector around. At first, I couldn't make out what was wrong but then I could see a golden retriever running around him, then when I was staring at him, I noticed that there was also a black Labrador and the pair of them were harassing him but not barking. I don't really know if they were attacking him or playing. All I was aware of was two dogs, but where's the owner? So, I stayed where I was. 'Carrottop' carried on up the hill. At the top of the hill there is a gateway into the field we were in, so what he did, he put his machine under the hedge, jumped over the gate and came walking down the road as bold as brass. So he had nothing to worry about. I made my way back to the hole in the hedge and waited for him to pass, as he passed I came through the hole and joined him and we went back down to the car. I said, what happened to the dogs, he said they just ran off. So, I said have you seen anybody, he said no, and neither had I. But we decided it wasn't worth taking the chance, so we drove off and as we passed the gateway, he jumped out and got his machine. We called it a night and went home.

On the next occasion, we went to Pugridge. On this particular site, we parked in the pub car park and then we ran across the road and jumped the gate onto the site. From the gate it's a track way that leads to the top of the hill and a small copse on the top. On the right hand side of the track is a small hedge but on the left, it drops away by about 3 feet into the field. This may have been the original Roman road. Anyway, we ran across the road and jumped over the gate and I started walking up. I stepped off the track and went down the slope onto the field, because you can find coins as you walk up. I heading for the top, which was a favourite spot of mine. Anyway, I turned around and 'Carrottop' was nowhere to be seen. By now, I was about half way along the track, so I got onto the track and looked down until I could see him. He was still near the gates but I could just about make out he was doing something with the machine. I later found out that what had happened was that before he had come out, he forgot to change the batteries and tried doing it in the dark; because as usual, he was half cut. So anyway, once I was happy with the situation, I carried on and I reached the top by the copse. Once you're there you're pretty safe, as there's lots of places to hide. So, whilst I was waiting for him to catch me up, I stayed in the shadow of the trees searching and as it happens, I found a rather nice Celtic bronze dove. As I was searching in the shadows, once again I heard him screaming and shouting. There was a little bit of moon and I looked down the track and I could see 'Carrottop' fighting off two Labradors again. I thought to myself, what the hell is going on here and then suddenly, I saw the headlights from a quad bike drive up to 'Carrottop' and I could see he was having some sort of argument or something. They turned round and started going back down towards the gates. This was the same way I wanted to go. So, I left from where I was standing at the top and went at a 45 degree angle across the field, so that I would end up further down the road as fast as I could. I ran down and then made my way back down to the car but there was no sign of 'Carrottop'. 'Carrottop' had not gone back to the car, he did the sensible thing. He didn't want the farmer to know where we had parked nor did he want them to get our registration number. So, I left the car park and drove slowly through the town, which is just down the road and there he was walking along the road. I stopped and he jumped in and he said "go, go, go, he's called the police." So, I went, went, went.

Back on the same site, this time McGiver, 'Carrottop' and I parked in the same usual spot but this time instead of going left and up the hill, we went right and down the hill towards the Celtic fields we knew. We went in on the site and everything was fine. McGiver found a quarter stator and 'Carrottop' and I found nothing. We had spent quite a few hours searching and by now we had had enough. So, we decided to go back to the field which we spoke about previously. So, we came out of the gate which was on the opposite side of the road and we ran across to the gate on the other side but we didn't go through it. We went into the trees and at this point, there's a wide hedge. Because we were going up the road but through the trees so we were not seen. Out the corner of our eye, we saw somebody. So, once we were in the trees, we stopped still so we could see what he was doing. Quite nearby is one of the tourist walking areas and we saw him go to a land rover parked in the area. He came out with two German Shepherds; fortunately, they couldn't speak English, haha. With his two dogs he went to the gateway, we think he thought we'd gone into that field. Because he stopped at the gate and did something I'd never seen before. His dogs had collars that had flashing lights, just so he knew where they were but I'd never seen this before. He was sending the dogs into the field, shouting fetch them. Once we had heard this, we started moving along the hedge as fast and as quiet as we could. Every time the dogs came our way, he called them back and sent them into the field, which enabled us to reach the car and scarper a bit sharpish.

Roman Disc Broach

10

Very Seldom Upright

'Twophones and I decided to go on the roast one night and after a tug of war, we made our way to the site where we met up with 'I-tie' and 'Trots'. On arrival, we were surprised to see that 'I-tie' and 'Trots'' cars were not there, despite having arranged to meet at a spot by the road in the aeroplane field. The aeroplane field is named because back in World War II, an American Flying Fortress had crashed on his way back from a bombing raid and had got all the way back to this field. His plane was shot and fell about 5 miles short of the runway at Bovingdon. Still to this day we are finding bits of it from where he crashed onto a Roman in Celtic site. It's a very hard site to work, you have to work your way through a bit of ally, bullets and various small bits of plane but in amongst all this crap are some nice finds.

We detract somewhat from the next escapade, so we go onto the site and start to detect. 'Carrottop' is drunk; not at the stage where he forgets his name and where he lives but just where he can still swing his machine, emphasis on the just. After about an hour, the time was roughly 11:45pm and the pubs had thrown out their last customers and 'I-tie' and 'Trots' arrived.

The corner of the field we call Corrine is relatively well lit because of streetlamps on the road. This meant the boys could make their way across the field to where we were and we could see them taking a zigzag route across the field, as they were out for lunch. We met up and had the compulsory smoke and chat communication, but held in an open field and not by a hedge as per usual. 'Carrottop' then farted so loud it rattled the feelings in my mouth. 'I-tie' then said who was that whereupon 'Carrottop' said you can have it if you want it. 'I-tie' out of his head started singing "I don't want it you can have it". Here 'Carrottop' and 'Trots' joined in. These three piss heads were in such fits of laughter they had just dropped to the floor on their arses still singing at the top of their voices. I was saying to them keep the noise down, bearing in mind we are on site behind the houses, a garage and pub.

Incidentally, the roast is also named after the pub. Then I walked away and carried on detecting, thinking that they were going to stop any minute. We were very wrong, instead they got louder and louder. They carried on for what seemed forever, so we quietly slipped off, but the boys were still sitting on the floor in a circle all the best you can with three people, singing their passes off. All that was missing was a campfire.

On another night, we were off to Mildenhall. Maguyver, 'Carrottop' and I, were present that night and on route we stopped off at an off-licence to buy some cigarettes. Unknown to me, 'Carrottop' had just bought a quarter bottle of rum and as we got back in the car he said I will get in the back. This was strange, as I thought he never gets in the back, he always likes to ride up front.

Mildenhall is about an hour and a half drive time from where we live, so about half way there, 'Carrottop' offered Maguyver a swig on his rum, which pissed me off, as 'Carrottop' knows I don't like people drinking when we go on hot sites because you need to have your wits about you when you're playing this game.

'Carrottop' sat in the back of the car and poured the whole bottle down his neck and that was well before we had reached the site, "too much too soon." 'Carrottop' had gone very quiet in the back of the car, because if you know him, he suffers from verbal diarrhoea when he has had a drink.

We reached the ancient woods at the top of the hill where we pulled in along the track way in order to get changed. I turned the car around in the driveway, parked up and started to get changed into my hawking uniform. These woods are pitch black at night, so Maguyver and I jumped out and opened the boot.

Where I had parked, there was a big puddle and I mean a big puddle at the back of the car. Maguyver asked me to pull forward a bit but me being me, said "no", I just wanted to get out onto the field.

Eventually 'Carrottop' mustered enough conscious thought to get out of the car and made his way to the boot. He was only able to do this by grabbing onto anything that was solid and between the back door and the boot lid.

I must say at this point in hindsight; what happens next is the funniest thing I've ever seen in my life, but it was one of those things that you had to be there in order to understand the comical side. At the time, I was livid.

So here we were standing at the boot of the car getting changed, the first thing that 'Carrottop' wanted to do was to put on his terrain monster truck running shoes (his Wellingtons) but this wasn't going to be easy. It's hard enough putting them on in your garden but when you're pissed and you have what appears to be Choice of 10 Wellington boots—there were only 2 but he was pissed and confused—it made things a lot harder. So with one hand on the car gripping it as if his life depended on it, he leaned into the car picked up some wellies and put them on the floor. After his third attempt, the boots were ready. Even with his vice-like grip on the rear wing of the car, 'Carrottop' swung around like a tree in a force seven gale.

After some effort and a few attempts he managed to slip off one shoe and placed an attempted short further into the welly, but missed completely and was now standing with one foot in a puddle. After a mammoth surge of energy, 'Carrottop' managed to get his sodden foot into his welly. At this point, 'Carrottop' now has taken a huge gasp of air and let out "my wellies are full of water." Maguyver snapped back with the comment "you silly cunt, you've been standing in a puddle of water." By now, I was dressed and was walking away in total disgust of him.

'Carrottop' shuffles around in the back of the car to where it was dry at the front. Here, 'Carrottop' has to face his next Herculean task; that's to gather up shoes and clothes and place them into the boot. Simple you might think, but we're talking about a man with the lights on when no one is home. 'Carrottop' is now leaning over the sill of the boot in an attempt to put his bits in and pull out his coat. This doesn't happen. 'Carrottop' has overbalanced and is now himself in the boot and not only that, 'Carrottop' has passed out there and there is no sign of life movement or anything.

Maguyver and I looked at each other in total amazement and he went over to the car as I am totally and utterly up my own arse about it. Maguyver carried 'Carrottop' and dumped him onto the backseat where 'Carrottop' just cannot keep any conscious thought process going and the light goes out; he is unconscious. 'Carrottop' keeled over like a parrot dying on a perch from upright to horizontal in one smooth action.

The next thing we have to do on this site is a "drop off". What this means is you drive around the road surrounding the site to a designated point where everyone bar the driver gets out and hides and the driver parks the car in a safe place and narks hack.

The drop off point on this site is a stile. The stile is the beginning of a footpath, so we leave the wood, which is approximately a mile and a half from the sty. On the way I say to Maguyver, "you are going to have to take the machines as 'Carrottop' is incapable of doing anything". We reach the drop off and Maguyver jumps out with machines while 'Carrottop' who has slightly recovered, fumbles his way out the back of the car and slams the back door. Slam is something you do not do. Normally you ease the door to the first click of the latch and whoever is driving would close it properly when he was safely parked up. Because 'Carrottop' had slammed the door, I sort of panicked and I shit my load actually and roared away.

As I was roaring away I looked in my rear view mirror just in time to see 'Carrottop' do a pirouette and fall on his face into the grass verge. I hadn't realised that once

'Carrottop' had slammed the door was still holding onto it in drunken stupor so I tore off and spun him up like a spinning top; his head must have been going place your bets as they do at a roulette table. I cannot stop to go and see what I had done 'Carrottop' bearing in mind that there are a few houses in this lane that I am in and foremost it is a HOT SITE.

I parked the car and made my way back to the others where we had agreed to meet on the field, which was under a big Sycamore tree that stood alone in the field.

When I arrive at the spot, 'Carrottop' is face down spread eagled under the tree and Maguyver is farting about with one of the machines, which turns out to be mine! I could see that he was trying to repair the stem that holds the search coil that had been snapped.

What had happened was Maguyver had handed the machine to 'Carrottop' and told him to hold them whilst he got over the sty, the idea being that once over the sty 'Carrottop' would hand the machines to him and allow 'Carrottop' to stager over.

'Carrottop' being 'Carrottop' when he is pissed; once he had the machines in his hands he would not give them up and in his pig headed way attempted to climb the sty himself. Once halfway over "yeah you guessed it" he fell the rest of the way, which resulted in my machine being broken, and another night fucked up over the devil's brew.

Maguyver and I dragged 'Carrottop' who is still passed out back to the sty and I went and got the car and we went home.

On another occasion, 'Carrottop' and I decide to go Silchester, where there is a "fuck off" Roman Fort, the walls are all intact and stand about ten feet high and all that is missing is the cap stones.

I managed to get 'Carrottop' out of the pub early and only half cut as again he had run out of money so he was semi-conscious which was not that bad for our 'Carrottop'. We made our way down to the site and there is a car park, which is wedged between the outside of the Roman wall and the lane.

The entrance to the car park is on a slight bend in the lane so if you park in the right spot you cannot be seen or lit up by the cars using the lane, which we did.

We got out and stood by the boot of the car getting our hawking uniform on, 'Carrottop' was standing nearest the hedge when a black Labrador dog and his accomplice, a Golden Retriever, burst through the hedge started to attack 'Carrottop'; not biting him which was a shame but barking and charging. The dogs had 'Carrottop' pinned up against the back of the car where he started to wave his arms about in the air and screamed at the top of his voice "GERTCHER".

This did the trick; the two dogs ran off into the night. These dogs were lovely; well-kept and fed, which meant that they were not strays.

'Carrottop' and I halted there for a while and waited for whoever owned them to come by but nobody turned up so we figured it would be safe to carry on.

We crossed the lane to work a little known Celt spot and spent roughly two hours of swinging stick on this site but had found nothing and decided to move to another field that was down the lane, which was part of the Roman settlement. So off we went; now this is a bit on the dodgy side as you have to walk down the lane with the stick in your hand and if somebody comes along, you're going to get "caught".

On the way along the lane you pass another car park that is in front of a small church. I don't like this car park as you cannot hide the car in there properly but about fifty yards further on and coincidentally at the beginning of the site. there is a foot path that takes you through the hedge and onto the field.

Once on the field you can walk along the hedge parallel with the road towards the opposite corner of the field, which is up a slope. In this far corner is the gateway that allows the farmer to gain access to his field but opposite the gate there is a bungalow. If you stay stealthy and quiet you can search there and it is one of the best areas for finding Roman coins.

When we got to this spot there were two other guys working the area and hawkers being hawkers went over to see who they were. I can't remember their names but as per usual 'Carrottop' knew one of them. Come to think of it he knew everybody; he should work for the missing persons bureau but anyway these guys were not from our manor.

We all worked this area for about two hours and I found thirty odd Roman coins and 'Carrottop' had found the same but none of them had anything to write home about. Although the area that 'Carrottop' was searching is sparse you do find the odd nice bit down there. Now 'Carrottop' needed at least one silver coin in order to buy the next night's beer and he was panicking.

I stayed were I was as I wanted quantity not the odd bit of quality. The three of us that were left up the slope were working close to each other, working the area in lines and now about half an hour had passed when night time silence was shattered with the sound of "GERCIIER".

We all looked up and the moon light we could see the golden retriever running up towards us. Now one of the two that I was searching with shouted to us "the farmer set the dog on us" and like three horses out of the trap we were off and running at top speed for the gate.

We hit the gate and straight over the top I went, as did the other two but now we were opposite the bungalow. The guys we met on the field and my car were at the bottom of the field; this meant that we would have to pass the farmer on his way up as we made our way down.

We had to move quickly, so the solution was to run down the lane but bent over as we ran as not to be seen over the hedge, can you picture that three men running down the road bent in half.

We ran and got to the first car park outside the church where these two guys had their three door hatchback, well they both jumped in the front seats and roared off wheels spinning leaving me standing there with nowhere to go.

After some serious contemplation if I went back to my car I would seriously be exposed and anyway where the fuck was 'Carrottop'? I had Oblivious flashbacks. I hid my machine in the hedge crept across the other side of the car park and hid in another hedge, the idea being if I was seen or caught they wouldn't find my machine.

There I am in this hedge having a smoke and waiting to see what pans out when this light bulb in my head, which was about the size of a sun rise in the Sahara Desert, turns on! "Yep the pennies dropped" these were the same two dogs from earlier and to add insult to injury, I thought I recognised that "GERCHER".

I retrieved my machine went back up the foot path and onto the field where I spot 'Carrottop' merrily swinging away who greets me with "those fucking dogs got me again".

We carried on for another hour when the two who had roared off returned to play. We told them the story where they laughed but I think they were severely pissed off under it all but that's Night Hawking for you.

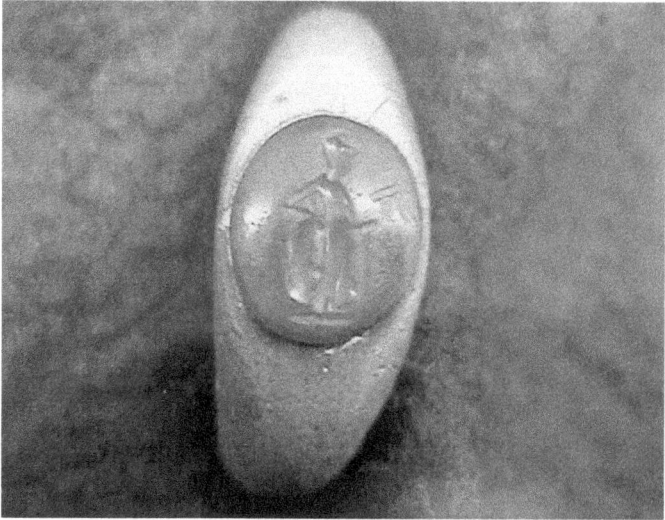
Roman Seal Ring

11

Bootsy

'Bootsy' and I go back a long way, off and on, we've been detecting for 30 years. He's the longest singular person I have detected with. But it started off very frictionally because we both came from different ends of the game. 'Bootsy' and his gang were all about making or earning money, where I was about coin collecting. So, this affected where we went and what site we went on. As I have said previously, we tended to meet up at 'Old Boy''s and decided where to go from there. The 'I-tie', 'Carrottop' and I would arrive in one car and 'Bootsy' and 'Pig' would arrive in another. They would have in mind where they were most likely to earn money, though this may not necessarily mean coins. Whereas I was only interested in coins and I always gave the Celts the priority. So, it took a few months of getting used to each other before the friction died off.

Probably just a coincidence, but I've only been caught twice by the Babylon and both times, it was with Bootsy. The first time being the Celtic site in my end of the woods called Bourne End. On this particular site, which happened to be on the top of a hill, a footpath ran along the ridge and one end of the footpath, there was a small housing estate, where we could park. So, we were working on top of the hill. From the top of this hill, if you look down one side, a small 'A road' ran past the site and the farm was in the corner of the field. So, the farmer could look out of his backdoor and if there was any kind of light, you could see us silhouetted at the top. I always searched down the side of the hill to stay off of the skyline but some of the others didn't bother. So, as a result, at some point we had been seen unbeknown to us. I was about half way down the slope towards the road and 'Animal' was further down than me. Suddenly, he came running past me shouting "cops". I turned to run and as I did, a huge spotlight was turned on me. I ran towards the footpath, taking the shortest route. Animal had gone at a 45 degree angle up the hill and as he ran, he alerted the others; even though the light would have done that anyway. I ran to the footpath and literally dived through the hedge. Once on the footpath, I could go left or right. Turning right led me up the hill towards my vehicle but I knew the copper wouldn't know which way I had gone, so that gave me a bit of breathing space. I stopped running and turned it into a fast walk. Huffing and puffing. I saw him shining his light up and down the footpath, trying to work out which way I had gone, so I had a good lead on him, so in order to get my breath, I eased back a bit. Unbeknown to me, another copper had followed 'Animal' up the field but not with a light. So, he effectively cut me off. I was walking up the footpath as quietly and as quickly as I could and I walked straight into him. Thinking I was going to attack him with my metal detector, he set about smashing it with his truncheon. Then the original copper came up the footpath and joined us and they marched me up the footpath to the top of the hill, there were one or two others with the farmer. I then learned that the others had escaped but had been stopped by a patrol car along the road. I wouldn't tell the police who they were and said I was on the field all on my own. They denied being on that field and said they had been somewhere else and then they let them go. After getting into an argument with the farmer over the rights and wrongs of the law, they decided to let me go but the officers took me back to the car where they did the various checks they do. Once they were happy the vehicle was legal, they then allowed me to be on my way. So, a bit of a spoilt night really, as not much was found from the short time we were there.

On the other occasion, again in my end of the woods, 'Pig', 'Bootsy' and I were on the Cow Roast (area). Once again this on the top of a hill. We'd been searching for a while, 'Pig' and I were more or less together whereas 'Bootsy' had moved across the field towards the hedge. I had found a quarter stator and was showing it to 'Pig'. More to the point, I was using his good eyesight to see if he could identify the coin. When suddenly we heard a car's wheels spinning and screeching, roaring off down the road. A burglar alarm then went off. Down one side of the hill, near the pub, there was a Porsche dealership and obviously someone had tried to break in or steal a car. The car had quietened down and we ignored it and then a helicopter went over quite low. 'Bootsy' had immediately run to the hedge and was hiding under it, unbeknown to us. 'Pig' and I were just finishing a cigarette and then the helicopter came around again and he started circling slowly around. Still the penny hadn't dropped at this point. Now we know they have night vision and infrared, so finally the penny dropped but it was too late. There was no point in running, as they were above us as we stood still. So, then he flashed what we could only describe as headlights and when we looked far down to the end of the field, we saw a car flashing its headlights. They were obviously signalling each other. As they did that, a huge spotlight came down on us. We were taking the mickey, pretending we were on the stage, waving our arms as though we were dancing and we just waited for the police to arrive. We could see them coming up the field and because of the railway line, which cuts up the site, they could only come from one direction. In any event, this is not a hot site, so we didn't really have anything to fear. So, when the police arrived, the same old usual questions, given what we were wearing and carrying, "what are you doing?" We were tempted to come out with all sorts of answers but kept it simple and told them we were metal detecting. When the officers had got their breaths back, they had just had a long run, and we started to talk to them quite amicably. We were putting two and two together and realised it was because of the Porsche garage. They asked us if we had seen anything or heard and anything, so we mentioned the car we had heard earlier on. Once they were satisfied that we weren't who they were looking for, they then turned their attention to determine whether we had permission to be here, as usual. Once again, a huge bluff was involved. As I had made inquiries to try and detect there with permission, I knew which farm and the farmer's name, so told the police and they went to the farm so they could ask. Getting to the farm isn't as easy as it sounds, as there are three farms up that road and the ownership could have been any one of them. So, the bluff was hoping they would not bother to investigate further; which they didn't. Two of the police officers escorted 'Pig' and I to my car and once again, they did the usual checks to see if everything was legal and then said we could go. Of course, we couldn't go, because now we had the problem of Bootsy. Now there was only one way across the railway line and that by the footbridge. So, instead of just driving off, we hung around the car, taking our gear off, hoping they would leave before us if we prolonged enough. Fortunately, they did and as soon as they were out of sight, 'Pig' jumped over the Sty and ran up the footpath across the footbridge to look for 'Bootsy'. He met him about halfway and they came running back and we were on our way. Although spoiled, it was not a complete waste of time, as I still had my quarter stator but 'Bootsy' had spent most of the evening under the hedge. That will teach him, for being a scaredy cat.

On one particular occasion, I went over to 'Bootsy''s house, 'Pig' was already there and we were deciding where to go. We agreed we'd go down to Tangmere. 'Bootsy' had heard the day before from someone else that the field had just been rolled and flattened, so off we went. We arrived down on Tangmere and popped up in our usual spot on the housing estate, walked across the first field to the main field. Now this brings us onto the spot where I told you previously that I had found a quarter stator after doing a boiler but this was before all of that time. When we got there, I thought we had walked into a rally, because sitting on the ground along the hedge in a line, there wers 15-20 people smoking and chatting and it was like a big reunion. I just wanted to get on a search. 'Bootsy' and 'Pig', who knew all of them, were sitting and talking to them and this went on for hours. All the time I kept searching, moving away from where they were and moved into the middle of the field. On a whole, I had a pretty good night. Not Celts but I had some Roman coins, one of which was a Denarii. So, I looked up and noticed a number of them were peeling off and going, so I walked back over to 'Bootsy' and 'Pig' and they said they were going now. I said but you haven't even turned on your machines yet. Even so, they wanted to go. They'd had a good social night, from what I could see and I was happy with my collection, so said fair enough and took them home. I'm just as bewildered now as I was then.

Of course, with 'Bootsy', it's not always about metal detecting, with him, it's treasure hunting in any form to earn money. There was another form of hunting and that's digging Saxon graves. You can see where the graves are from the crop marks of Aerial photographs but when you're on the ground, you can't see the crop marks. So, you have to find the graves, they are all laid out in one way. Head to the east, feet to the west. Once you find a grave, you can work out the head end from the feet end. The head end being the most important, as beads and broaches are found in that area; even the spears, the head of the spear would be near the head of the person, as the wood end would rot away. Even the shield would be near the chest area.

So the way this is done is that a long thin metal spike is pushed into the ground until you find an area where the resistance is less. Even though these graves are 1500 years old, you can still feel a lot of resistance when you hit the grave area. As it happens, 'Bootsy' is very good at this. I wouldn't rely on me doing it, as it does take quite a nack. So, once we had found an area that we were convinced was a grave we got to work, and incidentally Bootsy never got it wrong. We laid a big sheet out on the grass, next to the grave and then dug the earth out onto the sheet. One person going over the soil with a metal detector. Though it is mainly done by eye. The beads of course couldn't be found by a metal detector and the cord would rot away, except on one occasion when the binding was a thin gold strip. Although this has been broken by us digging, we did manage to retrieve most of the beads. On that particular grave, we also had a spear head and broach, there should have been two identical ones, but one was missing. There was also no shield boss. We were trying to work out if this was a warrior, as it was one half of one and one half of another. Maybe it was just a lady who had to have a spear. The other thing we expected to find, regardless of gender, was a dagger; which kind of indicates a juvenile or a teenager. Anyway, when you're happy that you've got everything you can, you then carefully refill the hole, taking all the earth from the sheet and replacing the turf, stamping it down as good as you can. Usually, within two or three days, especially if it rains, you'd never know a hole had been dug. We generally dig two or three of these excursions per year.

On a couple of occasions, when I was not there, they had had some really mega finds. Some broaches found were worth thousands of pounds. Another thing we did, is of course, hole digging on the fore shores of rivers. The favourite spot of course, is on the Thames at low tide near the old original London Bridge. With these holes, you have to go down quite a way. The ultimate depth being about 8 ft. These days of course, it has been banned and even if you get permission, which can be obtained, you can't go down more than 2 or 3 ft; which means you'd be lucky to even reach the Victorian layer. We used to dig down over the course of about three days, because the good stuff was way down. We would dig a whole about a metre square, when the tide came back in, we would put half a sheet of ply over the hole and a lot of rocks on top and then the next day when the tide was out, we just removed the covering and bailed out the water and carried on. A lot of coins and artefacts are found doing this. One of the main things that was sought-after were the Pilgrim broaches. Personally, I didn't care for them and was only interested in the coins which suited 'Bootsy', as most of the coins, unless they were gold or silver, he wasn't interested in. So, I kept the coins and he kept the broaches. I thought this was fair, as he did most of the digging. I just did the sieving. When he dug down, he did most by eye but then would dig out a shovel full of earth and put it into the sieve, which I would then sieve in the water's edge. When coins and artefacts aren't that far down, they come out as shiny as they were the day they were lost. So, really, the sieve was only used to get the very small stuff you could miss. Although, you still missed a few coins and we used to get a lot of pins. it's not that he missed them, he just couldn't be bothered with them. It would be virtually impossible for me to list all the items that we found, only outstanding ones. Sometimes, you would hit a spot that had not been dug before and you would get what is called a glory hole. What happens in the water is that you may get a big rock and as the current goes over the rock, you get an eddy behind it downstream. Items collect in these areas, which creates the glory hole. If you hit one of these spots, the pay-out can be really good. In one particular hole, we found 5 gold coins, these are called Anlett.

So, onto the next activity we did in different rivers across South East England. I've touched on this before, another harmless pursuit is bottle digging. Over and around Dagenham, a lot of rubbish was dumped in this area. So, there's a lot of bottle digging to be done. To this day, rubbish is still brought down the Thames to Essex. With bottle digging, there's not a lot of money to be had but the earlier the dig, the more likely you were to earn more money. The earlier bottles you find can go for a few pence. The money is in the printed and hand painted jar tops, which are quite beautiful. Even the old fish paste jars had lovely painted tops and the other thing was the old dolls heads, hands and feet. The rest of it, however, rotted away. If you could get these items, you could recreate a doll from the head, hands and feet. So, no real money to be earned but was a past time that could be carried out in daylight hours and was without the risk of being arrested. Again, we did hundreds of these, too numerous to mention all of them.

There was one particular activity that we did very rarely. On a tidal river in Kent, when the tide was out, you would get mud banks and these elevated mud banks originally were islands and originally, it was an area for Celtic pot making. But you had to be very careful on these islands, because the tide could come in and catch you out. Personally, I always took a rubber dingy with me, being a scaredy cat but once again, it was 'Bootsy' with his metal probe probing through the mud until he hit something hard. There were very few rocks or stones, so if you hit something, chances are it was a pot. So, then you dug down to retrieve the pot. Bearing in mind they had been in the sodden ground for 2000 years, these pots were very delicate and quite a few times, we'd puncture holes in the side of them. But if you could get one out undamaged, it became very difficult to preserve them. As they dried out, they became more and more fragile, to the point where just picking them up had them disintegrating in your hands. There are ways of preserving them, but the museum of London refused to tell us how. They said, we shouldn't have been digging them in the first place. In fact, the local council passed a by-law saying we couldn't go onto these mudflats. They actually have people patrolling there.

A One Off

We won a tender for the insulation of shower pumps in all the ensuites of a hotel in Bayswater. This geezer also owned a lot of houses and flats throughout the South East of England, which he rented out. When things went wrong in these properties, because of the area they are spread over, he would just use local geezers to fix the problem. We could see the possibility of a maintenance contract here. On one particular occasion, a tenant phoned him to say that her boiler had stopped working. She had had a local man in who had told her she needed a new boiler, but the price was quite high, so he told her to get a second opinion. She did that and he confirmed that a new boiler was needed. His price was very similar to the first one. So, we asked if we could improve on the price. Which we could by at least 50% and we'd still be in pocket. The job would have to be done very quickly, as this was a combi boiler, so not only did the lady not have heating, she had no hot water. I said I could do it the next day, so I bought the necessary materials, after extracting all the information I needed, and I left very early the next morning.

The job itself was in Brighton, so I realised I could finish the work and then travel along the south coast to Tangmere, a favourite site of mine. A Celtic site. So, with this in mind, I went off early in the morning, down to Brighton or near Brighton. The work went quite smoothly or okay and when I finished the job, everything was working fine and I left. By the time I had finished during winter, it was dark, so travelling along the coast was slow going. By the time I got to Tangmere, it was later than I thought it was going to be but anyway, I went. On this particular site, in the corner of this field, there was a lot of hot rock, which came before the other end of the field. So, I went to the first part of the field and there was no hot rock, no signals at all and I was able to walk along. I then approached the area of the hot rock and expected the machine to start chattering and make some noise. Suddenly, I got a reasonable signal, I bent down and found a Quarter Stator. Lovely. So, knowing that the hot rock was about to start, that meant walking halfway across the field, I decided to call it a day. I had got a Quarter Stator, I was over the moon, a simple in and out. So, I left very happy and drove home. Now from Tangmere to home, I knew that route off by heart and it's all backroads, so there was no problem in driving home. It was a nice and easy journey and a nice and easy find. What a lovely day that was.

A Missed Opportunity

The RAF has a Barracks at Mill Hill East which they disbanded. There were four big blocks of flats on the site which the local council were taking over and they embarked on a complete refurbishment. I won the tender for the first fix of the plumbing of the bathrooms and kitchens, and the removal and capping off to make the gas pipes safe. I started interviewing people, when I met Russ. Russ was older than all the other candidates and he learnt his trade in the army and he seemed the most trustworthy and reliable person. So, I took him on.

Now, the first fix of the bathroom and kitchen was a five day job, which left a day on the gas. I decided to do this personally. Over a few weeks, being there one day a week with Russ, we became quite good friends. Russ was an Anglo Indian but was married to an Indian lady. Like most squaddies, he liked his beer, which caused a problem in his marriage, which was why he was estranged from his wife. However, most weekends, either the Saturday or Sunday, and depending on the weather, he would take his boy to a junior nine-hole golf course. Eventually, my son and I joined him. We had good fun.

In one of the conversations, it came out that years previously, he was a bottle digger, and we arranged to go to a site that he knew one weekend. Unfortunately, the site had badly grown over and after a couple of failed attempts, we gave it up as a bad job.

I had been talking to him about metal detecting and he wasn't very keen, but he said he'd give it a go. I thought, if I went to a reasonably quiet site and he found some Roman coins, I could get him hooked. So, I took him to Bletchley. I purposefully went there early during daylight, so that I could show him the layout and explain to him what's what. The site is on a corner, so it's bordered by two roads. We drove up and down both roads and I explained to him where we were gonna go etc. The spot I had in mind was in the far corner of the one of the roads but bordered the other road. Because of the thick hedge, it was safe. However, driving up and down one of the other roads, the field opposite was also on the corner, as this was a five way roundabout. This field has always been grass with horses in it but as I drove past, I looked through the gateway and I could see that it had been ploughed. I was over the moon and got very excited, because this was a virgin field. Doing the safe site had gone out of my head.

The actual gateway was in the corner of the field and right next door there was a pair of cottages. We kept driving past because every time I tried to get a good look, there was always a car behind me. We went past a few times and that was our first mistake. Once I had satisfied myself with how to get onto the field, we went back to the big roundabout and went into the Little Chef and had a couple of cups of tea; waiting for nightfall.

Once it was dark, we couldn't walk down the road to the site, so we had to go to the original spot I had in mind. Here, we had to get through the hedge and across the road to get into the gateway. However, because of the thick hedge, the gateway was quite sheltered. So, once you were at the gate, anyone driving past was unlikely to see you. What the farmer had done was he had added timber onto the tops of the gates and strung coils of barbed wire across the top.

This made it very difficult to get over the gates. To the left hand side of the gates, was the field boundary. The field ran straight across past the boundary. Now I could see the danger, so I told Russ to go to the right hand side next to the hedge and work his way along there. I got through first and I turned right and got impatient. I started to search immediately. But as I explained to him, I had gone to the right and had walked 20 feet before starting to search. I looked up and I could see him standing there right in front of the gate. He was doing something, but I couldn't figure out what. Thinking we were fairly safe, I carried on down the hedge and thought to myself that he would sort himself out fairly quickly. I had gone about a third of the way down the field and oddly enough, still hadn't found anything, when suddenly, I saw the headlights of a land rover in the gateway. Russ was still standing in the gateway right in the middle of the lights. I heard the farmer shout to Russ to stay where he was, but I started to fight my way through the hedge. It took the farmer quite a while to get the locks off and get through. He could have just driven in.

Between the hedge and the road was a deep ditch. Fortunately, it was dry, so it gave me the cover to travel along the ditch without being seen. I went right to the end of the ditch and then ran across the road back to the Little Chef. I put my machine in the boot of my car and I took my barber off and then decided to walk down the road to see what was going on. I got about half way back when I bumped into Russ. Russ told me that the farmer had given him a damn good telling off and told him to get the hell out of it, as he was going to call the police. We just ran back to the car and left. On the way home, I asked Russ what the hell he was doing just standing there in the field. He had turned the knobs and couldn't get the machine to work. It was clear he had turned the wrong knobs. Because I had set the machine up, so all he had to do was to turn it on, but as we were in the dark, he clearly got mixed up. So, that was it, after that episode, for Russ there was no more metal detecting.

Anyway, the contract came to an end and Russ moved onto a really large one by someone else that he knew. We kept in touch and played golf on the weekends but after 2 years, he died of a heart attack. He was only 49. That's it really. Here's to you Russ, still thinking of you and miss you dearly.

The End

(Well I say it's The End and it is, of this episode anyway)
    PS; Oh! By the way did I forget to mention that in the fraternity of NightHawkers, I'm known as Seb!

Lightning Source UK Ltd.
Milton Keynes UK
UKHW012201070720
366166UK00001B/41

9 781728 353937